*The world of parents desperately needs this book. And no one
has earned the credentials to write it more than John Croyle.
A must read for parents.*

Robert H. Schuller,
author and founding pastor,
the Crystal Cathedral

*In growing up, my mother and grandmother were tremendous
role models in my life. Unfortunately, everybody does not have
that opportunity to have a family. But at the Big Oak Ranch
[with] John Croyle—that is a great organization trying to help
develop role models for young kids and give them
the childhood that they deserve.*

Charles Barkley, Olympic gold medalist
and former NBA basketball player

*Regardless of our status in life, the positions and titles that
we may hold, real success is based upon the relationship we have
with our family. Throughout my career I have dealt with thousands
of young men, and it's easy to see that the ones that have had the
advantage of a good home life and good relationships are much
more advanced and emotionally mature. As a parent and as a
grandparent, I want to know everything that I can about raising
children so I can help teach them to be a winner, and the book that
John Croyle has just written*—Bringing Out the Winner in Your
Child—*should be must reading for all of us because John Croyle
has made winners out of a lot of children.*

Gene Stallings, former head football coach,
University of Alabama Crimson Tide
and Phoenix Cardinals

Let me say what an honor it is to encourage all parents to get and read Bringing Out the Winner in Your Child. *I thank God for the four children he sent me, and I'm sure that the influence of the Big Oak family helped them be the successes in life that they were able to reach. The "Big Oak" formula for bringing out the winner in your child can be a great help to everyone.*

Bobby Allison, racecar driver,
Bobby Allison Racing Inc.

To my knowledge, no one seeks the neglected or abused adolescent and delivers such an effective work of redemption in their lives as Big Oak Ranch does. Instead of being paralyzed by the magnitude of what needed to be done, John simply made a start with a handful of kids over twenty years ago. He has continually multiplied that impact by increasing yearly the number of young people reached as well as the widening influence their lives have made on others.

Johnny Musso, former All-America halfback,
University of Alabama,
and running back, Chicago Bears

Not many people have had the opportunity to raise as many children as John Croyle has. At Big Oak Ranch children find love and acceptance, and in John Croyle they find a man who is able to lead them with a firm but gentle hand. John Croyle is a winner, and his proven, time-tested truths for bringing out the winner in your child make must reading for every parent raising a family today.

Clebe McClary, motivational speaker
and author of *Living Proof*

Bringing Out
THE WINNER
In Your Child

The Building Blocks of Successful Parenting

Bringing Out
THE WINNER
In Your Child

JOHN CROYLE

With Ken Abraham

CUMBERLAND HOUSE
Nashville, Tennessee

Copyright © 1996 by John Croyle

Published by
  Cumberland House Publishing, Inc.
  431 Harding Industrial Drive
  Nashville, TN 37211-3160

Cover design: Gore Studio, Inc.
Text design: John Mitchell

Library of Congress Cataloging-in-Publication Data
Croyle, John, 1951–
    Bringing out the winner in your child / John Croyle with Ken Abraham.
        p. cm.
    Includes Bibliographical references.

    ISBN 1-888952-25-3 (hardcover: alk. paper)
    ISBN 1-888952-90-3 (trade pbk: alk. paper)
    ISBN 1-58182-351-7 (trade pbk: alk. paper)

    1. Child rearing. 2. Parenting. 3. Parenting—Religious aspects—Christianity.
    I. Abraham, Ken. II. Title.

    HQ769.C955 1997
    649'.1—dc2l
                                                                96-5227
                                                                CIP

Printed in Canada
1 2 3 4 5 6 7 — 09 08 07 06 05 04 03

To my parents, Frank and Ruth Croyle,
who established the foundation;
To my wife, Tee,
whose heart has supported me with endurance and love;
To my children, Reagan and Brodie,
who have blessed beyond measure;
And to the thirteen hundred children
who have called Big Oak Ranch their home
and taught us these truths.
And most of all to God,
who forgives, forgets, and enables us all.

Contents

	Acknowledgments	*xiii*
	Introduction	*xv*
1	A Dream Come True	3
2	Eighteen Years to Pack a Suitcase	25
3	Four Things Our Children Need to Know	33
4	Where Are the Boundaries?	49
5	How to Set Realistic Boundaries	67
6	Children Want Discipline—Really!	95
7	Why Are We Afraid to Discipline Our Children?	109
8	How to Apply Discipline with Love	129
9	It's Okay to Say No	151
10	Children Listen with Their Eyes	175
11	Quality Time Never Comes	193
12	Take Me Out to the Ball Game	211
13	When to Intervene in Your Child's Affairs	227
14	Keeping on Course	245
15	The Joy of the Journey	255
	Notes	*269*

Acknowledgments

*T*here is no way to adequately say thank-you to all the children and staff who have given their very lives to make a difference in the life of a child. And to the many friends of Big Oak Ranch who have been so committed to believing and investing in these past twenty-three years.

Nor can I properly say thank-you to the mentors, leaders, role models, heroes, and good friends who have influenced my life since the early days in Gadsden, Alabama, until this very day. The really great thing about having good friends is the comfort in knowing that they know you and love you in spite of your faults. They also know who they are and need no special acknowledgment because that is what makes them your friends. But from the core of my heart I say thank-you for loving me and my family and for being there through the tough times and the great times.

Introduction

*M*AYBE THE KIND of person you are, or once were, is not the kind of person you want your child to be. I can relate to those feelings. Regrettably, I have made almost every mistake a man could possibly make as a husband and as a father. I have failed my family and myself in more ways than I care to mention. I don't make this statement lightly, but with remorse and shame.

Thankfully, though, there came a time in my life when I knew I did not want to continue traveling down the wrong track any longer. I realized that in some ways, though I had the best life could offer, I was not what I was supposed to be.

This change of heart and mind was not the result of any earthshaking spiritual experience. I was not visited by an angel; I did not hear God's voice speaking to me out of the sky; nor did a traumatic event trigger my transformation. I simply recognized that I was going in the wrong direction, and I needed to make some drastic changes in my life. I called out to God for help, and He responded by forgiving me and helping me turn around and to get on the right track.

Maybe you have messed up in the past as a husband, wife, parent, or simply as a person. Everybody messes up, but the wise person recognizes he is going in the wrong direction, stops, turns around, and gets on the right side of the road. It is never too late to change. If you are not the kind of person you want your child to be, you can start today to be that kind of person. If you will ask Him, God will forgive you too and help you to be the person He created you to be.

Your mate will notice the difference and so will your children. Don't get discouraged if your family members do not notice immediately that you have changed; they will. In time, as your actions become more consistent with your heart, they will recognize that you are becoming not only the parent you have always wanted to be but also the person you have always wanted to be as well.

As a good friend of Big Oak Ranch, Dr. Robert Schuller often says, "When you think you have exhausted all possibilities, remember this: You haven't!" I know it is possible to change. If God can change me, He can change you. We are all in this growing-up process together.

Being willing to change your parenting habits is the first step to *Bringing Out the Winner in Your Child.* Join me in the quest.

Bringing Out
THE WINNER
In Your Child

1

A Dream Come True

"WATCH IT! Something moved in there!" The surprised railroad worker slid open the door to a large, supposedly empty boxcar the men were preparing to load.

"I see it!" one man said in an excited whisper. "What is that?"

"Shine a light on it," said the first worker.

It was a cold, rainy October morning in Gadsden, Alabama, and as the burly railroad worker pointed his flashlight into the boxcar, a chilling wind whipped through the car. Dust particles swirled in the beam, making the light look like a long, probing dagger, extending all the way from the rail worker's hand to the recesses of the large boxcar.

What the workers saw at the end of that light beam was even more chilling.

In the corner of the ice-cold boxcar huddled a shivering little boy. He was clutching a can of beans, a can of sauerkraut, and a near-empty box of cereal. In a feeble, terrified voice, he cried, "Go ahead and shoot me. I don't care!"

Two railroad workers quickly climbed into the boxcar and knelt next to the boy. "Son, what are you doing here? Are you all right?" one of them asked.

"Get a blanket!" one worker called to the others outside. "Let's get him into something warm."

The men took the boy from the railroad yard to the security office, wrapped him in blankets, fed him some hot soup, and called the local police.

A brief investigation soon revealed that the boy had been living in railroad freight cars for seven months after running away from his home in the northeastern part of the United States. When the police attempted to contact his parents, they discovered that his father was gone and his mother did not want him. He had no family in the area and nowhere to go.

"What are we going to do with him?" asked one of the officers.

"I know where we can take him," another of the officers replied. "Let's call John Croyle."

———

When the telephone rang at Big Oak Ranch in nearby Glencoe, I answered.

"John, we have found an abandoned little boy here at the railroad yard," the chief security officer informed me. He went on to explain the details of the situation.

"I'll be right there," I answered, reaching for my jacket almost before I hung up the telephone. I hopped into my car and pointed it toward Gadsden.

I arrived at the security office and was introduced to a little boy named Bobby. I was appalled at Bobby's pathetic condition. He was filthy, his clothes were tattered, and he looked as though he hadn't eaten a square meal in a month. His emotionless eyes looked like those of an animal that had been severely beaten.

I put my arm around Bobby and said softly, "Come on, buddy. You look like you need to eat." I took the little hobo back to Big Oak Ranch, fed him, clothed him, and cared for him as though he were my own son. Big Oak Ranch became Bobby's home. The principles you will discover in this book helped to change Bobby's life and the lives of hundreds of other children. These principles can make a difference in your parenting, as they have in mine.

ECHOES FROM THE PAST

Answering that call from the security office was an echo of the call I had answered several years earlier. Actually, I have felt "called" to care for children for most of my life. A tragedy in my own family placed a passion in my heart to help hurting children.

When I was five years old, my four-year-old sister, Lisa, and I were playing on the tombstones during a funeral Mom and Dad were attending at a cemetery near our home. Lisa and I were playing on one large grave marker, and I jumped off and bounded to another stone. About three minutes later, I heard a dull, sickening thud. I whirled around and, to my stark terror, saw a sight I will never forget. The large tombstone had fallen over, pinning my little sister's chest to the ground. Blood was pouring out of her mouth and nose. We later learned that when the stone fell on top of Lisa, the crushing weight of the rock thrust two of her ribs through her heart and two of her ribs through her lungs.

I stood there speechless, paralyzed with fear. I didn't know yet what was wrong, but I knew it was serious.

From the grave site, Mom and Dad saw what had happened. They rushed across the cemetery to where Lisa and I had been playing. My dad pulled the heavy stone off my sister's frail body, carefully picked her up, carried her to the car, and placed her on the back seat. "Get in!" he cried out to Mom and me.

Mom hurried into the front passenger seat, and I scrambled onto the back-seat floorboards. Dad stomped on the gas pedal and headed the car in the direction of Boaz-Albertville Hospital.

Kneeling on the floorboards, as the car sped toward the hospital, I watched Lisa's lips and eyelids turn dark purple. Her face turned pale. She was dying.

At the hospital, my dad sat next to me in a chair and said, "Lisa has gone to heaven."

"Well, when is she coming back?" I asked innocently.

My dad sadly explained, "Lisa will be living in heaven forever."

DISCOVERY OF A GIFT

Lisa's death made me emotionally tough, but it also ingrained upon my heart an indelible concern for other children. Throughout my school years, I always wanted to do anything I could to help give kids a chance. My dad, Frank Croyle, began coaching kids in Little League, softball, and basketball. Not only did I greatly benefit from his expertise, I soon wanted to emulate it.

Athletics always came easily to me; I especially loved football and basketball. By my senior year of high school, I had received all sorts of athletic scholarship offers from colleges around the country. Growing up in Gadsden, as I did, there was no question in my mind where I wanted to play. Like most high school football players in the state of Alabama, it was my dream to play for the famous football coach Paul "Bear" Bryant, at the University of Alabama.

I played defensive end for the Crimson Tide for three years, from 1971 through 1973, during which time we had a 32–4 won-lost record and we won the Southeastern Conference Championship three times. My senior year, we landed atop the United Press International poll as the best team in the nation, and I was named UPI second-team All-American.

————

During my college years, I spent the summers working at a children's ranch in Lumberton, Mississippi. I started as a counselor to the boys. After my sophomore year, I went back as the head of ranch maintenance. By the time I had concluded my senior year of college, I was ranch director. Although I carried a passion to help children, little did I know how I was being prepared for my future position.

After my first summer working with children, I sensed I had found my calling. One of the first confirmations came when I was only nineteen years of age. As a camp counselor, I met a young boy who came to the ranch straight from the streets of New Orleans. The boy's mother was a prostitute, and he was the banker and timekeeper for her "business."

At camp that summer, I made a special point of befriending that little boy. Just before he returned to the seedy underbelly of New Orleans, I had an opportunity to talk to him about changing the quality of his life and his relationships with other people. The boy listened carefully but was reluctant to respond. I didn't push him or try to coerce him in any way.

I simply told him that I loved him and that I would be praying for him.

The following summer the same boy returned to the ranch. When he and I had a chance to talk privately, he recounted verbatim the information I had shared with him the previous summer. I realized then that even though I was nothing special, I had a gift to help children.

After that, the thrill of sacking a quarterback or clogging up a hole at the line of scrimmage and preventing a big play paled in comparison to the desire developing within me to create the best children's home in America—a place where abandoned, abused, emotionally scarred, and broken kids could find a home, hope, and unconditional, no-strings-attached love.

TIME TO CHOOSE

Throughout my college career, Coach Bryant kept tabs on my dream of opening a children's home. Once, between my freshman and sophomore seasons, I stopped in at his office to discuss the idea again. I told The Man—as his players respectfully referred to him—about my work at the ranch in Mississippi during the summer. The excitement I felt about my newfound passion was contagious. Just about the time Coach Bryant was really getting interested, there was a knock on his door.

A secretary came into the office and said matter-of-factly, "Coach Bryant, I have Vice President Agnew, Bob Hope, and Roone Arledge of ABC Sports all on hold. What should I tell them?"

In his usual gruff voice, The Man answered, "Tell them I'll be right with them."

Coach Bryant looked back at me, and with a hint of a smile, said, "Now, tell me about this ranch you want to build." By his actions, Coach Bryant made me feel like a winner. I have never forgotten his example of putting me first and giving me his undivided attention. I have tried to follow his example with my own children and the children of the ranch.

Toward the end of my senior football season, I went again to talk with Coach Bryant privately. He was aware that I had received some interest from National Football League teams and was feeling out my interest in professional football. I wanted to know how Coach Bryant sized up my potential for a career in the NFL. Personally, I wasn't sure I even wanted to make the leap from college ball to the pros. Standing at six feet, six inches and 215 pounds, I was fairly light for a college defensive end. The linemen in the pros dwarfed me. Besides, my knees had been severely damaged during my career at Alabama and I wasn't sure they could endure the constant high-impact collisions that I was certain to encounter in the NFL. More important, I could not shake the notion that I had been called to build the best children's home in America.

Maybe I can do both, I thought. *Maybe I can establish the children's home by playing professional football. After all, most pro ballplayers receive a substantial salary. Maybe I should play pro football just long enough to make the money needed to finance the children's home.* I took the idea to Coach Bryant.

When I told Coach Bryant my idea, he was noticeably apprehensive. He listened intently, then rubbed his chin for a few seconds (I thought it seemed like an hour). Finally, he spoke in a soft, slow drawl, "John, don't play professional football unless you are willing to marry it."

I was thinking about marriage all right, but certainly not to a piece of pigskin pumped full of air. I was stunned by Coach Bryant's words. "What do you mean, Coach?" I asked.

"Your heart is not in playing professional football. Your heart is with that children's home you keep telling me about. Forget about pro football, and follow your dream. Go build that children's home, and I promise, I'll help you every way I can. I'll write you a letter of endorsement. I'll even serve on your advisory board of directors, if you want me to."

I left Coach Bryant's office a bit shell-shocked by his unanticipated response but excited about the confirmation I felt in my heart that he was right. I wasn't called to play pro football; I was called to build a place where hurting children could find help.

LOCATION, LOCATION, LOCATION

I started looking for a piece of property to purchase, but the pickings were rather slim—especially since I had a grand total of five thousand dollars in the bank, a gift I had received from the local well-wishers in Gadsden. They had held a day in my honor (it was legal to do so in 1974), to welcome me back home from Tuscaloosa. One day, my dad told me about a beautiful spread of land for sale outside Gadsden. We drove out to look at it, and I knew the moment I saw the property that it was the place for which I had been searching. A small farmhouse sat in the middle of a 120-acre plot, the perfect location for a ranch-style children's home.

The owner of the property was not quite so convinced.

Maybe he thought I wanted to open up a reform school-type home, or perhaps he was afraid I might bring rough-housing boys to the area and create problems for his former neighbors. For reasons he did not reveal, he was not enthusiastic about his land being used as a children's home. To discourage my interest, the owner offered me a conditional deal. He would sell the land to me if I could raise the fifty-thousand-dollar down payment—within forty-eight hours!

Dad and I left our meeting with the landowner and I immediately called a friend, an oral surgeon in Birmingham, who I thought might be able to help me raise the money.

Amazingly, he did not hang up on me. Instead, my friend offered to contribute fifteen thousand dollars! I was already up to twenty thousand dollars! In my mind, I had one foot on the property. But I still needed thirty thousand dollars, and the clock was ticking. My chances of meeting the forty-eight-hour deadline seemed bleak.

Then I had a surprise encounter with John Hannah, a former Alabama teammate. He had known about my plans to build a children's home, and John believed the plans could be accomplished.

The last time I had seen him, his parting words to me had been, "See you in the pros." Since then, John had been negotiating with a pro team. I, on the other hand, was having enough difficulty negotiating with a local landowner. When I told him about the property I wanted to purchase for the children's home, he offered to contribute the money he was to receive as a signing bonus to my cause. The bonus he received for signing was thirty thousand dollars.

I bought the property and named it Big Oak Ranch, a place where children could have a chance. The name came from a verse I had read in the Bible: "So they will be called oaks of righteousness" (Isaiah 61:3). I named our first home for boys in honor of my friend. The dream was about to come true.

THE FIRST FIVE BOYS

In 1974 the United States was in the midst of an energy crisis, resulting in gas shortages, skyrocketing fuel prices, and long lines at the gas pumps. Unemployment and inflation were high, as were interest rates. Our nation had recently endured the disheartening divisiveness spawned by Vietnam and Watergate. People were not in a trusting mood. It was not an atmosphere conducive to taking risks. Even my mom asked me not to pursue my dream of building the children's home.

Nevertheless, I was convinced that the need for a children's home far exceeded the risks of opening one. I moved onto the property and lived in the old farmhouse in the middle of the ranch. Word about the home for boys spread quickly around the Gadsden area, and before long, I had five boys living with me. Bobby, the boy found in the railroad boxcar, was one of the first.

Another boy was brought to me who had no responsible living relatives. He had nowhere to go, so I took him to live with me.

A third boy came to me. He had been adopted, but his mother had grown tired of raising him and virtually threw him out of the house. The boy was living in a barn before he came to Big Oak Ranch.

The fourth boy was living in a house that might as well have been a barn. His parents had abandoned him, and he was trying to keep warm by covering himself with cardboard boxes. When the social workers found him asleep in his bed, they had to brush the snow off before they could pick him up.

Not all of the first boys who came to Big Oak were poor. One boy came with his parents, both of whom drove Mercedes-Benz automobiles. They had all the material things modern society equates with success. But they didn't have a clue how to raise a teenager. They asked me if I would be willing to work with their son and raise him. I said sure, and the boy moved in with the four other boys and me.

———

Those first five boys went with me everywhere—even on dates. I was courting my wife-to-be, Teresa Smith, whom we all started calling "Tee." During those early days of Big Oak Ranch, Tee and I always had five young "chaperons" with us.

More than once, we went to a drive-in movie, and I looked over at her and asked, "Baby, would you like some popcorn?"

Five heads would pop up from the back seat and say, "Yes! And we'd like a Coke too!"

The boys were our family. When Tee and I married, our boys attended the wedding. Fortunately for me, Tee loves kids as much as I do, although neither of us really knew what we were getting ourselves into when we said, "I do." Any newly-wed couple is bound to have adjustments to make, but imagine adapting not only to a marriage partner but to an instant family of five boys, all teenagers!

It was tough in those early days. I didn't know much about parenting. I was only five years older than several of the boys! We were always scraping to find enough money to feed and clothe them. We ate a lot of peanut butter and jelly sandwiches in those days. We got used to stretching a shoestring budget as far as it would go. Little by little, we acquired more children, as well as houseparents, staff, and facilities.

LIFE ON THE RANCH

Since officially opening Big Oak Ranch in the fall of 1974, we have given a home to more than thirteen hundred children.

Many young men and women whose lives had been spinning out of control are now stable, productive members of society.

People often ask me, "How many of the children at Big Oak Ranch were abused or neglected before coming there?"

My stock answer is, "All of them, in one way or another."

My staff and I have found children living in junked cars. Others we have pulled out of their own grime and excrement. One little boy's mother had dipped his legs in a vat of hot grease as a punishment. On more than one occasion, I have had parents drive onto the ranch property, open the car door, push a child and a sack of clothing out the door, and then speed off, without ever saying a word.

In some obviously abusive situations, I've asked for some of our kids. I go to whoever has custody and talk to him or her about the program at Big Oak Ranch, promising to help raise the child to adulthood. I do it because I figure the children ought to have a better life.

More important, I see every child as a winner. For instance, when Tim first came to us at Big Oak Ranch, he had been rejected by his birth parents and then thrown out by his adoptive parents. Nobody wanted anything to do with him. Throughout his entire life he had been told he was not worth a thing. Few people can be told they are worthless over and over and not believe it. Tim was no exception.

When I first saw Tim, I saw a boy who did not care about anything or anybody. But I also recognized that Tim had natural abilities and untapped potential—if he could only begin to see himself as a winner instead of a loser. During Tim's time at Big Oak Ranch, we concentrated on helping him see his God-given potential. He came from making straight F's to B's and C's in a short time because he viewed himself as a winner. The boy who came feeling worthless left Big Oak as a young man focused on the future.

One day while I was eating lunch at my favorite eating place, Pruetts Bar-B-Q, a young man in his late twenties stopped by my table. I recognized him immediately as one of our "sons" at the ranch. I hadn't seen him for several years. He was now a grown man.

"Tim!" I said, as I stood up and shook his hand. "How in the whole wide world are you?"

Tim looked at me and said with a smile, "I am married. I have a great wife and two great kids and a good job. I'm taking care of my family because of Big Oak Ranch. Thank you."

Tim's words were worth more to me than all the money or fame in the world. Over the years, I have seen the Super Bowl rings now worn by many of my former Alabama football teammates who went on to the pros and won the game's biggest prize. And those rings are impressive. But nothing can compare with the joy in my heart when I know I have invested in someone's life. Helping a child who once thought he was worthless to become a winner far exceeds any temporal, material reward gained in any arena.

———

No matter what the circumstances, or what the child's attitude, I choose to see the potential winner a child can be if only given a chance. That is the fundamental philosophy behind everything we do at Big Oak Ranch.

Today at Big Oak Ranch, our children live eight to a home—not dormitory—with a husband and wife as full-time houseparents, in a comfortable two- or three-story house. As much as possible, we try to create a normal family atmosphere in each home. The family unit is central to everything we do at Big Oak Ranch. It is where the children learn to give and receive love, many for the first time in their lives. The boys and girls in each family are between the ages of six and eighteen. We feel everyone needs an older brother to look up to and also know what it's like to take a little brother under his wing. We all need a hero.

The houseparents are in charge of raising the children, administering normal everyday discipline, and providing heavy doses of love and fun—just as all children wish their experience at home could be. The houseparents maintain strict rules, and the children are expected to obey them. Usually they do. Why? Because obedience is expected. When kids don't obey or are extremely rebellious, they are brought to see me. Rarely do I paddle a child. Paddling an abused child is like throwing a match into a raging forest fire. It is just more of the same. But there are other ways to get a child's attention, without raising your voice or laying a hand on the child. I will be describing some of those methods later in this book.

Early to Rise, Early to Bed

Each child's day at Big Oak Ranch begins around 5:30 A.M. and ends at 9:30 P.M. Every day starts with devotions and chores before school. The younger boys help around the home, and the older boys work on the ranch, taking care of the property and the animals. We raise our own beef, pork, and chickens, as well as some vegetables and hay for our horses.

The boys' ranch now includes two fishing lakes, a large swimming pool, a children's center with athletic facilities, and a softball field. We have dogs, horses, pigs, cows, and approximately three hundred chickens. The boys' ranch is a bustling place, especially after the children come home from school. After school, most of the kids have chores to do. Participation and doing your share are part of being a family. Some of the boys band together to gather hay, wash cars, work in the huge garden, or tend livestock. Each child gets an allowance for doing his work, but he gets docked a dollar for every minute he's late to work. If there is one thing we try to teach our children, it is how to be prompt!

Some of the children who first came to us were not accustomed to working. Stevie was such a child. One day, Stevie came running into the ranch house screaming, "I'm dying! I'm dying!"

"What's wrong, Stevie?" his worried houseparents cried.

"I'm dying!" Stevie repeated even more emphatically. "Look at this!" he said as he wiped a foreign substance from his forehead.

It was sweat.

Since then, Stevie has learned the value of hard work, and the intense satisfaction that comes from a job well done.

WHAT ABOUT THE GIRLS?

I had no intention of ever developing a similar program for girls because I knew absolutely nothing about helping them. But then I met a twelve-year-old named Shelly. Shelly had been raped by her father while her mother held her down.

I went to the courtroom and asked the judge to allow me to take her home. The judge knew about our successful program for boys at Big Oak Ranch, but he also knew that we did not have similar facilities for girls. He refused my request. Shelly was sent back home to live with her parents. The next time, her father not only sexually abused his daughter, he killed her.

When I learned of Shelly's death, my stomach knotted so tightly I could barely breathe. I made a promise to God that when the time was right, we would build a home for girls. In the fall of 1988, we opened Big Oak Girls' Ranch and now have five fully functioning homes on a 325-acre piece of property in Springville, Alabama. The program for the girls is almost identical to the boys' program.

BEAR CARE

Coach Bryant was true to his word. He not only became a believer in Big Oak Ranch, but he also joined our advisory board and became one of our biggest supporters. He was never bashful about promoting the Ranch. The afternoon before the 1982 Liberty Bowl, when Coach Bryant would coach his last game, an enthusiastic fan thrust a commemorative T-shirt through the crowd and shouted, "If you will sign this, I'll give a thousand dollars to any charity you name!"

Coach Bryant reached for his pen and replied, "Send the money to Big Oak Ranch." In my last conversation with Coach Bryant before he died, he asked me if the man had sent the money. He had.

Ray Perkins became Coach Bryant's successor as Alabama's head football coach before going on to coach in the NFL. Coach Perkins also became convinced that what we were doing at Big Oak Ranch worked in the lives of children. One day when Coach Perkins was visiting Big Oak, he admired the houses in which our children live. He casually asked me what it cost to build each home. I told him that the current cost was sixty-seven thousand dollars.

We talked further as we toured the grounds. Suddenly, Coach Perkins spied a buckskin-colored horse in our pasture.

"I'd like to have a horse like that," Coach Perkins told me.

"You would?" I answered quizzically.

I couldn't imagine why a man such as Coach Perkins would want one of our horses, but I was extremely grateful for his support of Big Oak Ranch. I immediately said, "He's yours—we'll give him to you."

Coach Perkins shook his head and said, "No, I can't allow you to give him to me. Let me buy him."

With a twinkle in his eye, he took out his checkbook and wrote out a check for sixty-seven thousand dollars. Today eight boys live with their houseparents in the Ray Perkins Home.

No Strings Attached

The ranch receives no government money; we have not asked for any, nor do we want any. We operate entirely from private donations. Nevertheless, like all families, we have to find funds for food, clothing, dentist and doctor bills, lessons, and all the other expenses that are involved in raising a family. We are just like any other family except we have more children!

Sometimes the pressures of parenting get pretty intense. When that happens, I recall a lesson I learned from Coach Bryant. He was the master at getting a player to ignore the pain from aching ribs or a cracked hand. He taught us that when our opponent thought he had us whipped, there was still some fight left within us, and all we had to do was call on it.

Many parents I meet nowadays are right there. They feel discouraged and defeated in their relationships with their children. They want to be good parents, but they don't know where to find that "something extra" within. This book is meant to give you some positive principles that will help you find that something within. Then you in turn can bring out the winner in your child.

What Is a Winning Child?

We have found that a child who possesses the following traits or characteristics will, most of the time, move into adulthood with a winner's heart. A winner is focused on the right goals, is full of character and integrity, has courage, has the ability to say no when he needs to, has good work habits, is solid in his decision-making processes, is flexible yet uncompromising, unselfish, motivated to be the very best he can be, is committed to God, and is a leader because he knows how to follow. Most of all I think a child with a winner's heart is one who has been trained with loving discipline in a firm yet consistent home by parents who are committed to helping the child reach his or her potential. Obviously this is the result of a team effort.

All I Know Is What Works

Besides helping to raise more than thirteen hundred children, somehow my wife, Tee, and I found time to have two wonderful children of our own. Our daughter, Reagan, is now in her late teens, just starting college. Our son, Brodie, is in his early teens and in the midst of junior high school. All of the same principles Tee and I applied in raising our Ranch children have been home-tested with our own two children. It has not always been easy for our children to share their mom and dad with so many others. But Tee and I knew the example we set was having an impact when a number of years ago I brought home a six-year-old boy who had been severely abused.

I carried the boy to the bathroom of our old farmhouse on the Boys' Ranch and ran some water in the bathtub. Tee and I prepared to give the boy a warm bath. I took off his shoes, which were much too small and had frayed the skin on the boy's ankles from the friction of rubbing blisters. I gently pulled off the child's shirt when Tee and I were taken aback in horror and disgust. Obvious signs of child abuse showed on the boy's stomach, back, and ribs. We carefully placed the boy in the tub, and as gently as possible, attempted to wash out his wounds. When we were done, I picked him up and stood his battered body on the bathroom vanity as we patted him dry and wrapped him in a towel.

Just then, I heard a sound behind me. I turned and looked, and to my surprise, I saw five-year-old Brodie holding a stack of clothing. He had gone to his room and gathered an assortment of his T-shirts, underwear, and pajamas. He held the clothes out toward the bruised and hurting little boy, who seemed to be about Brodie's size.

"You don't have any clothes," Brodie said to the boy. "You can have mine."

Brodie dropped his clothing at the boy's feet. About that time, nine-year-old Reagan came in and said, "Come here, buddy. Let me take care of your cuts."

We took the little boy out to the kitchen and let him sit on the counter. There, Reagan and Brodie helped Tee dress the boy's cuts and bruises, applying antiseptic medication and sterile bandages.

As I stood watching the spectacle in our kitchen, I thought, *If Tee and I can continue to teach our children to love in such a manner, then our lives will have been a success.*

Granted, you may never have to answer a call to go retrieve a battered, abused boy or girl, but we are all called to be examples to our children. We are all charged to model love. We are all charged with the responsibility of imparting meaningful, lasting values to the next generation of children. Our example will always outlive our advice.

YOU ARE NOT ALONE

Parenting sounds like a big job . . . and it is! The good news is: You are not alone. You are not the only parent with questions and concerns about parenting. Similarly, you are not the only parent to have days when you wonder why you ever had kids in the first place. Perhaps you fear you are doing a poor job of preparing your children for life, or you feel you should be doing better than you are. *I must be doing something wrong,* many parents think, *or this parenting thing would be easier.*

The truth is, you are probably already doing a pretty good job at parenting—otherwise, it's likely you would not have opened this book. Or maybe you have been going through some tough times with your children, and you are hoping, *There must be another way to go about this!*

In any case, take heart. It is important for you to know, right from the top, I have never met a perfect parent. You are not a perfect parent, I am not, nor were our parents. Moreover, most of us have spent a great part of our adult lives seeking to forgive, overcome, or otherwise deal with hurts from our own childhoods. No wonder we have trouble being good parents; we are not even sure we know what that means!

Most of us began our parenting journey with a naive idealism, rooted in a deep love for our children and a sincere dedication to doing our best to "raise them right." Before long, however, something went wrong during our parenting adventure, and we found our feelings of optimism fading into friction, frustration, and anger at our children who did not seem to cooperate with our ideas of success and happiness for them.

You may have started out with high hopes for raising healthy, well-adjusted children, only to discover that the job is much more challenging than you ever dreamed. And no one informed you in advance of how constant, time-consuming, physically and emotionally draining, and all-encompassing parenting can be. Unfortunately, few practical handbooks on parenting have been available until recently. When you left the hospital carrying that beautiful baby, nobody handed you a guide to raising successful children.

Now that you are immersed in the complicated task of parenting, you may feel at times that your best efforts have been in vain. After rocking your children until they were too big to hold, wiping their runny noses, reading stories until you were hoarse, running all over town to every conceivable school, church, or civic activity, you may be dismayed and disappointed to find that your children remain immature, selfish, and seemingly unaffected by your massive doses of love.

Take heart. You are not alone.

Admittedly, the fact that we are all in the same sinking ship may not be all that encouraging to you. On the other hand, this book is sort of a lifeboat. This lifeboat has a lot of patchwork done to it, because Tee and I have made a lot of mistakes. We have hit every type of wave, underwater mine, or cataclysmic storm imaginable in our adventures in parenting over thirteen hundred children. What remains is a lifeboat we know will stay afloat. If your boat is sinking, jump into ours!

Or better still, allow this book to help you discover where the leaks are located or may develop in your boat.

And remember: Even in the best boats cracks develop. The best boats still require regular maintenance, checkups, and occasional overhauls. The boat is yet to be made that can be put out to sea and allowed to sail perpetually. Every vessel requires constant service to maintain seaworthiness. Similarly, there has never been a perfectly prepared parent, one who needs no further reminders, ideas, or techniques.

Top quality airplane engines are often taken apart after about five thousand hours of flight, even if no defects are discernible. Although the engine may be running fine, it is torn down, completely checked over, lubricated, and then put back together. After all, it is better to know that the engine is running well than to simply assume that everything is going well. How much more should we periodically "tear down" the attitudes and actions involved in parenting, give them a good going over, lubricate them with a fresh infusion of love, and put everything back together to continue the journey? That's what this book can be for you: a chance to get a new perspective, patch up some problem areas, be fortified within, and become the parent you have always wanted to be.

Consequently, you can have hope that your parenting will help bring out the winner in your child. This book and its principles will work for you, wherever you are in your parenting journey and no matter how late in the process you are getting started.

It is never too late to start doing right. *There is always hope!* If your children are already grown, maybe you will have the opportunity to teach your grandchildren positive principles for living. Perhaps you and your adult son or daughter can sit down and talk about things that maybe you should have packed into their emotional suitcases—things your adult children had to learn the hard way or from someone else. Similarly, if you are the product of poor parenting, determine that you are going to build on what your parents did right, and do your best to forgive them for and overcome those areas where they failed. The cycle of poor parenting has to stop. Let it stop with you.

No investment we make in life is more important than the values we teach to our children. A hundred years from now, it will not matter what size home we owned, the kind of car we drove, or the amount of money we had in the bank. But the world will be different because you and I were important in the life of a child.

Come on and join us as we share some practical, down-to-earth ways you can help bring out the winner in your child.

THE WINNER'S FOCUS

1. How would you describe a good parent? What are some areas in which you feel you would like to be a better parent?

2. Describe the circumstances surrounding the birth of your children. Were your children "wanted" or "planned"? How have those circumstances influenced your attitude toward parenting and the way you treat your child?

3. Nowadays, headlines bombard us with news of child abuse and child abandonment. To what do you attribute the increase in the occurrences of parental misconduct toward their own children?

4. In what ways has your adventure in parenting turned into a nightmare? A dream come true?

5. Often the tragedies that strike our lives can either motivate us or paralyze us. How have the hurts in your life helped to shape you into a better parent?

2

Eighteen Years
to Pack a Suitcase

*T*HE MOMENT YOUR CHILD is born, a "suitcase" is opened inside his or her heart, mind, spirit, and soul, in that innermost place of being. This spot is the very core of your child's existence. When he or she leaves the warm, nurturing environment of Mother's womb and enters the cold, often hostile world, you and others close to the child begin to pack that suitcase, the bag he or she will carry throughout life.

Initially, your child's suitcase is wide open and empty, with plenty of space to pack life's experiences. But it soon begins to fill. Everything you provide for your child goes into that bag, the good things—good clothes, good home, quality education, good work habits, strong moral and ethical values—as well as the bad things—bad attitudes, bad habits, bad feelings. Even residual guilt that you may be carrying as a result of your relationship with your own mother or father may subtly transfer to your children. All of this ends up in your child's suitcase. On the other hand, if we are not careful, it is sometimes easy to neglect packing some essential qualities such as character, courage, commitment to God, and ability to discern right and wrong.

PACKING FOR THE BIGGEST GAME OF ALL

Having the chance to play football for Coach Bryant at Alabama was exciting. I will never forget getting ready during the week for an upcoming ball game. Besides the drills and scrimmages, we reviewed game films of our opponents and even computer printouts listing every conceivable statistic on their strengths and weaknesses. Whether playing a regular conference game or the national championship in front of millions of television viewers, it was always a big game as far as Coach Bryant was concerned.

On Friday afternoon following the final preparation practice before a road game, we packed our large, green duffel bags—sacks big enough to carry all the equipment any football player needs. First into the bag went our shoes, either cleats for playing on natural grass or soft spikes similar to tennis shoes for playing on artificial turf. Then we would toss in our assorted pads for the various sore spots and bruises our bodies acquired during the long, brutal season. Then came the thigh pads, knee pads, hip pads, shoulder pads, chest pads, helmet, socks, supporter, and jerseys. We'd pull our bags shut, then get on the bus and go to the airport with the equipment.

Arriving at the opposing team's stadium, we'd go to the locker room and unpack our duffel bags, and begin to get ready for the big game. Everyone was psyched, ready to get out on the field. Imagine the horror, then, when one of the players got completely dressed, ready for the game, and suddenly realized he had forgotten to pack his helmet, the most essential piece of equipment of all!

Life is like that. It is always the big game. There are no scrimmages or preseason practice games. This is the real thing; this is the big time, and we must pack our children's bags with the essentials for whatever they encounter.

Many children are sent into the game of life unprepared, ill-equipped, and not ready to play. Granted, you can play without all the pads, but no parent in the world would expect their son or daughter to play in the rough-and-tumble game of life without the most essential piece of equipment of all.

What is the most essential equipment our children need for the game called life?

A child's most essential piece of equipment is a solid value system, from which spring virtues: good habits, courage, honesty, integrity, perseverance, resolve, commitment to God, and, in a word, *character*.

THERE IS ONLY SO MUCH TIME TO PACK

Your child's suitcase begins to fill up quickly during the first six years of life. Estimates suggest that 85 percent of a child's character is established before the age of six. By the time your child is ten, his suitcase is already quite full. Sometime between your child's tenth and fourteenth birthdays, an alarming yet inevitable phenomenon begins. The suitcase slowly begins to close.

Some people call this period the "turbulent teenage years," because this is when conflicts over independence begin to escalate. Whatever you call it, this is a period when a parent's influence usually begins to pale compared to the powerful pull of your child's peers. Beyond that, the media and other external influences, both positive and negative, are affecting your child. Many of these influences not only can but do lead our children in the wrong direction. Often these external forces deposit items in our children's suitcases that we wish weren't there but are almost powerless to remove.

By the time your child reaches fifteen, the suitcase is closing still more rapidly. Often this is a period of parenting most of us would rather skip; it is frequently the time when any rebellion that has been smoldering below the surface in our teenager's life suddenly erupts like a volcano! Many parents step back, aghast, and say, "What is this? Where in the world did that attitude come from?"

In fact, that same attitude has been building in intensity for years and the parents did not realize it until this explosive confrontation.

During this time, your children may challenge you about the length, style, or color of their hair, how much or what type of makeup they can wear, or what is an appropriate dress length. Children will want to wear T-shirts sporting all sorts of unusual slogans; fashions and styles will be a constant point of contention. Thirty years ago, who would have thought that boys would wear earrings, or that body piercing and tattooing would be considered an art form?

Certainly, the issues precipitating parent-child confrontations may change, but the confrontational attitudes packed in your child's suitcase will be determined by the relationship you have with your child and how well you have packed those bags. For example, when a two-year-old says, "Shut up, Mom!" it may seem amusing to family members and friends, but it is a serious problem you must confront and correct because ten years later the same words ring hard in the home and heart when your twelve-year-old shouts defiantly, "Shut up, Mom!" This time the words resonate with the rebelliousness of a teen whose suitcase is missing some essential pieces of equipment but whose bag is drawing more tightly closed every day. Same words, different attitude. Or was it? Maybe that attitude was packed in the child's bag a long time ago, And then, one day, it happens. The suitcase closes shut.

As parents, you and I can never be quite sure when this day will come. But I guarantee, under normal conditions, by the time your child has reached senior status in high school or has moved off to college, that bag is virtually shut. We may still exercise our parental authority and as parents we will still have influence, but be assured the time for packing the suitcase has expired. Whatever you and I have put into that suitcase, bad as well as good, is permanently stored for future use or misuse.

Certainly there are other influences in our children's lives: media, music, movies, television, teachers, friends, classmates. But you and I as parents are charged by law, by our own family values, and by the Creator who made us, with the primary responsibility of preparing our children for life.

To Prepare or Not Prepare

Well, Mom and Dad, we have defined the problem. Now let's fix it. An error does not become a mistake until you refuse to correct it. Are you doing your job packing your children's suitcases with all the essentials? Are you going to prepare your child adequately? Are they going to have all the necessary equipment? Have you included the helmet to protect the vital organ of the brain? Will the breastplate and shoulder pads be there to give him security and safety when the opposing enemy delivers a forceful blow?

Consider the lasting impact you have on your children's lives, because good or bad, essentials or nonessentials, attitudes and ideas are filling up their suitcases, increasingly by influences over which we have little control. And remember, we have at most eighteen years to do our job. It's an important job, and if you don't do it, others will, but the results will not be what you might hope.

Parents, what's it going to be? Remember: Our children

are on loan from God for only eighteen years. We have no time to lose. Let's get started!

The Winner's Focus

1. What essentials should we pack in our children's suitcases? What do our children need to flourish and be successful in life?

2. They are called "the teenage years." The process is called "growing up." To Mom and Dad it means their job is nearly through. If you are looking for motivation, consider this: If your boy is a sophomore in high school, you only have him home another 730 days. Your daughter is nine? She and her suitcase will be gone in 96 months.

   Calculate how much (or little) time you have left with your children in which to influence them for good. Write that number down in your business calendar, or post it in that place where all truly important reminders belong: on the refrigerator door. Every time you see it, remind yourself that the days are numbered, and they are slipping away rapidly. Let's make every day count with our children.

3. If we are not careful, we can work so hard to give our children things we didn't get while we were growing up that we sometimes forget to give them the things we did get: lessons such as the importance of respect for elders, looking adults in the eye when speaking to them, the value of a good day's work for a good day's pay, respect for other people's property and for those people who are different from us in race and economic or educational background.

4. Society today is full of "adult children" living in thirty- and forty- and fifty-year-old bodies whose bags were not

properly packed by their parents. It is very difficult to pack something in someone's bag that was never packed in yours. Integrity, honesty, honor, commitment—hopefully you learned these values from somebody. If you haven't, how can you teach them? If you have not developed strong values in your life, now is the time to start. You must realize your own weaknesses or lack of values and work on them so you can pass them on. If you have been blessed with good role models, learn to appreciate their contribution to your life, and pass it on. Someone showed you, now show your children and others.

5. Sometimes things are packed in our bags that we do not even realize are there until we stop and think about them. Ask yourself, *What have I learned from a mentor that I want my child to learn?*

Who taught you how to tie your shoelaces? Who taught you how to ride a bike? Who taught you how to tell time? Who taught you how to drive an automobile? Most of us can remember the people who taught us these or similar things. But who taught you the essential things? Who taught you how to get up when you were knocked down? Who taught you how to treat other people fairly? Who taught you how to have a relationship with your mate? Who taught you how to live with integrity? Who taught you how to be disciplined in your lifestyle? Who taught you how to console a friend who lost a loved one? Who taught you how to love a child?

Much of what we have learned, whether positive or negative in our lives, you and I have learned from people around us, by watching them, studying them, listening to them. Remember, the student always watches the instructor much more closely than the instructor watches the student.

- Who taught us to tell the truth? Who taught us how to lie?
- Who taught us how to have confidence? Who taught us to cower in fear?
- Who taught you how to be a man or woman with virtue? Who taught you to be a man or woman with weak, vacillating values?

Mom and Dad, you and I must remember the good things we were taught and the lessons we learned from our mentors so we in turn can teach the good things to and weed out the bad for our children. Remember, if your children don't learn the positive from you, they will learn the negative from someone else.

6. Name five people who have most affected your life. How did each one influence you? What lesson did you learn? Is this something you want to pack in your child's suitcase? Think about what you have learned and how you can transfer that truth to your own son or daughter.

7. It has been said that a problem well defined is 90 percent solved. You and I as parents sometimes have to take off our rose-colored glasses and look at our children and admit, *Maybe there are some things I still need to pack in my child's bag that I have forgotten or didn't realize were essentials.*

Now is the time to get started. Begin today by attempting to pack one vital value in your child's suitcase. Make a list of what character qualities you deem important and necessary to prepare your child for the game.

3

Four Things Our Children Need to Know

W HEN CHILDREN COME to Big Oak Ranch, they are usually scared and hurting and feel abandoned, alone,
unsure, confused, or angry. More than likely, they have come
from extremely negative circumstances and have been abused
in one way or another, either physically, verbally, mentally, or
emotionally. This sort of pain is no respecter of persons,
whether the family comes from a lower socioeconomic background or from the wealthiest of homes. Nor are these feelings
the exclusive property of our Ranch children.

All of our children are trying to find something they can
hang on to; others are trying to find something they can reject.
Regardless, when my staff and I meet with a new child at the
Ranch, I look the child square in the eyes, whether an eight-
year-old little girl or a fifteen-year-old young man. Invariably,

I tell them four things. These four things are ground rules so our children will know exactly what is expected of them and what will be delivered by us as their "parents." Notice: Our children must know what is expected of them, and we as parents must deliver. Success in parenting hinges on these truths.

Unconditional Love: I Love You . . . Period!

First, I look our child right in the eyes and say, "I love you." Many children nowadays are not accustomed to a grown man expressing no-strings-attached love to them. In our Ranch children's pasts, most of the time, when an adult said, "I love you," the adult wanted something from that child. Or there was some other kind of price tag on the adult's expressions of love. Love always had a price. Do your children sense there is a price tag on your love, that as long as they are good, you will love them?

When I look our children in the eyes and say, "I love you," it is simply to let them know that we operate differently in this family. The basis of our relationship is going to be unconditional love, no strings attached, no matter what. Our goal is to help that child succeed by building on a foundation of love rather than fear.

Your children also need to know beyond a doubt that you love them. They need to understand that your love for them is unconditional. It does not depend on whether they win the big game, become cheerleaders, get great grades in school, or anything else. It is relatively easy to express your love when your children are doing well; it is tougher, but more crucial, to express your love at those times when your children fail or let you down.

In his book *What Kids Need Most in a Dad*, author Tim Hansel relates a personal story of his parents' unconditional love following one of Tim's greatest triumphs and one of his worst failures. Tim's mom and dad sacrificed many personal pleasures and both worked two jobs to help make ends meet in their family. As a high school student, Tim was the president of the student body and an outstanding high school football player; he was voted to the all-state team. The night Tim's team won its final game, several of the players decided to celebrate—a bit too hard. Let's have Tim finish the story:

Somewhere we had gotten some beer, and according to our high school logic, we thought that the more we drank the more we were celebrating. We drank too much.

A policeman happened to drive by and spot us in a parking lot behind some stores. Doing his job, he came over to investigate and discovered that more than a few of us were quite thoroughly inebriated.

The policeman put in a call for some help. Then, in my opinion, he started pushing around some of my friends. Because I was student body president, I felt it was my job to defend them, and I ended up trying to wrestle with the cop. That was not a good idea.

The next thing the cop called for was a paddy wagon. Twenty minutes later we were all on our way to jail. That night was one of the longest I've ever spent. At about five the next morning—just about the time the newspaper was being delivered to our home with my picture in it for being an all-state athlete—my parents received a phone call from the chief of police.

"Mr. and Mrs. Hansel, are you wondering where your son is? I'm phoning from the city jail, and I would like you to come down here and pick up your son."

I can imagine how long that drive downtown was for my folks. When they arrived, they saw a group of dejected young men. Other parents also arrived and had to face the same kind of disappointment. Their sons, who just a few hours before had been a source of such great pride, had all failed so miserably.

My mom and dad walked in, and I'll never forget the moment when their eyes met mine. They must have been wondering if all their sacrifices had been worth it. But they never spoke a word.

We got in the car. The sun was coming up and tears were rolling down my cheeks. Finally, I could take the silence no longer and blurted, "Aren't you going to say something, Dad?"

After a pause that probably seemed longer than it really was, my dad finally spoke. "Sure. . . let's go have some breakfast, *son.*"

Those were the only words he uttered. At a time when I had failed him most tragically, he reminded me that I was his son. At a time when I felt the deepest remorse and a total failure, he said, in effect, "Let's get on with it."

In the years that followed, he never once brought up that incident. He simply continued to love me for who I was and who I could be.[1]

The response of Tim's parents is a great example of unconditional love, love that does not depend on the actions of the other person. Let your children know that you love them—period! Beyond that, let them know that there is nothing they must do to earn that love. Nor is there anything they can ever do that will destroy your love for them. This is not to say that you neglect to discipline your children, or that you are not grieved when they do poorly in school, do something wrong, or disobey your instructions. But it does mean that your children know that you are going to love them no matter what happens.

TRUTHFULNESS: I WILL
NEVER, EVER LIE TO YOU

Second, I tell our new children at the Ranch, "I will never lie to you." Because our children have been deceived and manipulated so frequently before coming to us, most of our newcomers are totally unsure if there is anyone they can trust. Devastation due to lying is not unique to abused or neglected children. Your children's trust in you can be just as easily destroyed should they catch you in an obvious untruth. Gary Smalley shares what happened to a young man in his book *The Hidden Value of a Man:*

> A child's heart is easily bruised. Easily broken. And once seriously damaged, no surgeon can repair it. Only the Almighty Himself has the skill to restore its original balance, potential and capacities.
>
> Recently, a 40-year-old man described a Saturday morning 28 years before that nearly stopped his heart and is still affecting him today!
>
> I was just 12 when my Boy Scout troop planned a father son camp-out, he said. I was thrilled and could hardly wait to rush home and give my dad all the information. I wanted so much to show him all I'd learned in scouting, and I was so proud when he said he'd go with me.
>
> The Friday of the camp-out finally came, and I had all my gear out on the porch, ready to stuff it in his car the moment he arrived. We were to meet at the local school at 5 o'clock and carpool to the campground. But Dad didn't get home until 7 P.M.
>
> I was frantic, but he explained how things had gone wrong at work and told me not to worry. We could still get up first thing in the

morning and join the others. After all, we had a map. I was disappointed, of course, but I decided to make the best of it.

First thing in the morning, I was up and had everything in his car while it was still getting light, all ready for us to catch up with my friends and their fathers at the campground. He had said we'd leave around 7 A.M., but he didn't get up until 9:30.

When he saw me standing out front with the camping gear, he finally explained that he had a bad back and couldn't sleep on the ground. He hoped I'd understand and that I'd be a big boy about it but could I please get my things out of his car? He had several commitments he had to keep.

Just about the hardest thing I've ever done was to go to the car and take out my sleeping bag, cooking stove, pup tent and supplies. And then, while I was putting my stuff away and he thought I was out of sight I watched my father walk out to the garage, sling his golf clubs over his shoulder, throw them into the trunk and drive away to keep his commitment.

That's when I realized my dad never meant to go with me to the camp-out. He just didn't have the guts to tell me.

How do you recalibrate a child's heart after it has been damaged by a dad's broken promise?[2]

I could recount dozens of sad examples of young people who have experienced serious doubts about trusting their parents because of inconsistencies. I'll summarize a few that might sound a little too familiar:

- Thirteen-year-old Steve wonders if his parents are truly the upright citizens they pretend to be. The reason for Steve's doubts? Steve knows for a fact that his parents lied on his school registration forms. Steve's parents wanted to get him into a school with a reputation for better academic performance than schools in surrounding districts. To make Steve eligible for that school, his parents said that they lived in a town within the school district. They listed a friend's address on all the school registration forms.

  Steve's cooperation was required to maintain their ruse. He could not, after all, tell anyone where he actually lived and had to use the fake address any time he completed any forms at school. Steve probably received a better education in the better school district, but the awful price his parents paid for it cannot be measured in test scores or dollars and cents.
- Brandon knows that his parents used false income figures to get a home loan. He has heard his dad boast about how he "beat the system."
- Sarah wonders about her mom's truthfulness. Frequently when one of the family members answers the telephone and the call is from someone with whom Sarah's mom does not want to talk, she instructs one of the children to tell the caller she is not there. In a similar situation, Billy's dad insists that he does not want to lie, so he actually steps outside his house onto the porch after telling Billy to tell an unwanted caller, "He just stepped out. He should be back soon."
- Seventeen-year-old Josie knows that her dad lied on his job résumé. She knows because she typed the document on her computer for her dad so he could print multiple

copies, changing the information as he felt necessary for each prospective employer.

Your children will notice any inconsistencies between what you say and the way you actually live. Children have an uncanny gift to spot a phony! Your inconsistencies will undermine your credibility. They will also destroy your opportunity to discipline your children, especially in their teenage years, when they begin to question your authority. As fourteen-year-old Chris said when he was caught lying about whether he had been smoking marijuana at a junior high school dance, "What can my dad say to me? He lies to people every day on his job. He's a salesman and he would tell a customer anything to make a sale. Besides that, I smoke my dope, he drinks his. What's the difference?"

With our children, it is important to establish, up front, that we are not going to lie to them. We do not always have to tell them everything they want to know. In fact, a child can develop a sense of insecurity if the parents provide too much information too soon for the child's maturity level. (For example, I feel it is poor judgment to explain the birds and bees to a five-year-old child because she is not equipped emotionally or any other way to handle this information.) Nevertheless, our children must have confidence that we as their parents will never willfully say something that is untrue. We should reiterate to our children in every way possible, "I will never, ever purposely tell you something that is not true."

Telling our children the truth has important ramifications for discipline, rewards, and keeping our promises. If we establish a high level of consistency in our words and actions, our children will soon discover that they can count on us to follow through with what we have said, whether that results in something positive or negative. For example, when we tell our child, "If you come home late again, I am going to take away your driving privileges," we must do what we said, even if it is difficult or inconvenient.

On the other hand, when we tell our children, "If you clean up your room, I will take you swimming this afternoon," we must keep our promise. Otherwise, our children will quickly realize that our words do not carry any weight; they do not have any real meaning. A broken promise is a lie to a child.

Later in this book, we will look more closely at the importance of keeping our promises. For now, please understand: When we as parents commit ourselves to speaking the truth in love, we provide a grid that lets our children know that if they do something negative they are going to be dealt with negatively; if they do something positive they will be dealt with positively. Consistent truth-telling on the parents' part sets the ground rules for honesty on the part of our children.

SECURITY: YOU'RE STUCK WITH ME!

The third thing I tell the new children at Big Oak Ranch is: "I will stick with you through thick and thin." This lets the children know that they have a future, and perhaps most important, it lets them know they have someone who will be there for them. Whether they realize it or not in their young minds, this reinforces the fact that they are of such immense value that someone is willing to stand in the gates of hell and fight for them.

Ideally, both mother and father should emphasize their commitment to their children. Unfortunately, in the real world that is often too much to hope for. Many children have already experienced the pain of their parents getting divorced. Others are latchkey kids who see their parents only a few hours each week. Many children have grown accustomed to having an absentee father even when the father is living at home! For some children, that is the only sort of daddy they have ever known.

Consequently, even if you are the only one in your family who is willing to make such a commitment, or if you are a single parent, it is imperative to impress upon your child that you will be there for him or her.

Danielle and Stephen experienced a loud, tumultuous marriage that eventually ended in a bitter, resentful divorce. Unfortunately, their nine-year-old son, Alex, was caught in the middle of the mess and was not shielded from the couple's hateful remarks and actions. One night, after the divorce was final and Stephen had moved out of the house, Danielle was tucking Alex in at bedtime.

Alex looked into his mother's face and said bluntly, "Daddy went away. Are you going to go away too, Mommy?"

With tears streaming down her face, Danielle promised Alex that she would be with him until he was a grown man. And she has stayed true to her word. Danielle attends all of Alex's Little League games and all of his school programs and functions. She takes him with her everywhere she goes. In short, Danielle is pouring her life into her son.

"Sure, I get lonely sometimes," she says, "but I have only a few years left to help Alex. I want to be there for him as much as I can be. If that means I have to set aside my own plans and desires for a while so I can spend the time with him, I want to do it."

Even in marital separations and divorces with minimal bitterness, Alex's question is still a concern: "Are you going to leave too?" Divorce creates insecurity in a child's mind, but even single parents can bring out the winner in their children. Many great men and women owe their success to that one parent who said, "I will always be there for you."

CONSEQUENCES OF DISOBEDIENCE:
DON'T DO ME WRONG! I'LL GET YOU!

The first three truths our children need to know are all very positive. They provide plenty of that warm fuzzy feeling that we all desperately need. By our words and actions, we are giving our children emotional support, truth, and endurance. We are assuring them that our relationship with them is one of security, longevity, and a solid base on which to build.

Now, get ready to shift gears!

The fourth thing I tell every new child who comes to us at Big Oak Ranch is, "If you do me wrong, I'll get you." This sounds harsh, but we want our children to know that there are boundaries within which their conduct is acceptable, and if they cross those boundaries, they will be dealt with accordingly.

I want our children to always wonder what I mean when I say, "If you do me wrong, I'll get you." At that precise moment when they are tempted to do something wrong, I want them to see the look on my face and realize the seriousness of the consequences they will suffer if they choose to commit the offense. Are they willing to commit the act knowing that there will be negative consequences equal to their actions? I want them to hear my voice in their heart, saying, "If you do me wrong, I will get you."

Certainly, our aim is not to strike fear into the hearts and minds of our children; nor should we be overbearing taskmasters. But there is nothing wrong with our children having a healthy respect for their parents. Thirty-four hundred years ago, God instructed children in Exodus 20:12 to respect and honor their parents. That principle will still work today if we will encourage it. Consistent correction and loving discipline are basic to our daily job description as parents. Our children need to know that if they disobey, there will be specific consequences.

Furthermore, they need to understand that the measure of their discipline will be commensurate with the offense. For example, if they forget to make their beds or they leave clothes lying on the floor when they go to school in the morning, those are minor infractions of our house rules, and the children will receive mild reproofs. But if they begin to smart off, talking disrespectfully to their parents or other adults, or if they have a bad attitude and are generally rebellious, then we increase our discipline to match the offense. Should our children commit felonious acts, such as stealing a car or some other major crime, we deal with that according to the laws of the land. We do not attempt to shield him or her from the consequences of the actions. It hurts sometimes, but children must learn that there are limits to how far they can go.

It is important that parents learn to align the discipline of their children with the circumstances surrounding the misdeed. For example, Joey, an eleven-year-old boy who lived at the Ranch, crept into one of our homes and stole a package of hot dogs. He darted outside and ate the whole package of raw hot dogs before anyone saw him.

When we found out about Joey's offense, we had to take into account why he did what he did. Was he stealing for the thrill of theft? Was he stealing because he was hungry? Or did he steal the hot dogs because when he was younger, before coming to Big Oak Ranch, he would sometimes go two or three days without food?

Prior to coming to live with us, Joey never knew when he was going to have another meal. When he saw the hot dogs, because of his past conditioning, it was almost instinctive for him to steal food to eat. Obviously, we did not discipline Joey for taking the hot dogs in the same way we would have dealt with a mischievous vandal.

With your children, you must carefully consider the reason behind their actions before lashing out in arbitrary or universal discipline. Our children are all different, and every circumstance is different. All of these factors must be weighed before administering discipline. Never discipline your child when you are angry. Anger clouds our judgment.

PAINLESS DISCIPLINE

Please understand, when I speak of discipline, I am not talking about beating up your children. On the contrary, corporal punishment, although effective with some children, is often an exercise in futility with many others. At times corporal punishment is necessary, but when to use it is always a judgment call. Instead, depriving a child of some privilege the other children are allowed to enjoy is frequently a much more effective means of bringing about constructive change in a child's conduct and attitude.

Once we had a boy who was always disrespectful to his elders, no minor infraction where we live. Big Oak Ranch is nestled deep in the foothills of northeast Alabama. In our part of the country, young men and women are expected to address their elders as "sir" and "ma'am." The proper answer to a question is not simply yes or no; it is, "Yes, sir" or "No, sir," "Yes, ma'am" or "No, ma'am." Such archaic terms may not be important in some parts of the country, but in the deep South, we think these terms show respect to our elders and other authority figures.

Tommy, however, was not from the South. Nor did he see any reason to address his houseparents or other staff members at Big Oak as "sir" or "ma'am." In fact, he refused to do so.

Tommy had been with us for only a few days before our long-anticipated trip to Six Flags Over Georgia, an amusement park near Atlanta. As some staff members were busily packing the vans, other staff members walked around the

Ranch to gather all the boys together in one of the homes. We didn't want to miss anyone.

When all the boys were assembled, I shouted, "Is everyone ready?"

"Yes, sir! " the boys shouted in return. Everyone was pumped up and looking forward to a great time at Six Flags.

Just as the boys began to pile into the vans, I suddenly raised my arms high in the air and shouted, "Wait a minute!" The boys stopped in their tracks.

As seriously as I could muster, I announced, "Everyone goes except the boys from the Hannah Home."

"What?" a collective cry erupted from the eight boys who lived with their houseparents in the Hannah Home. "Why can't we go?"

"Well," I began speaking slowly, knowing that the boys were hanging on every word, "it seems that Tommy is having a hard time learning to say 'Yes, sir, No, sir, Yes, ma'am, No ma'am.' We have warned Tommy a number of times, but it doesn't seem to be sinking in. So because Tommy refuses to get with the program, his house, the Hannah Home, will not be able to accompany us on our trip to Six Flags today."

One of the older boys, a leader in the home and a quality young man, asked if we would give him and the other boys from the Hannah Home two minutes with Tommy in private.

I said, "Sure," and the staff members and I walked out of the room. We listened carefully to make sure that nothing abusive was done to Tommy. The other members of the Hannah Home had quite a conversation with the young boy!

When the staff members and I returned to the room, a few minutes later, Tommy walked up to me and said, "Mr. John, sir, I promise, sir, from now on, sir, I'll say 'Yes, sir' and 'No, sir' or 'Yes, ma'am' and 'No, ma'am' every time I am spoken to by an adult, sir. I guarantee you; I promise, sir."

I smiled at Tommy as I said, "Get into the vans, you boys from the Hannah Home. You too, Tommy." From that day forward, until the time that boy left Big Oak Ranch several years later, he never forgot to use "sir" and "ma'am."

To some people, our way of dealing with attitudes such as Tommy's might seem cruel or unfair, but it sure got Tommy's attention, and we never had to lay a hand on him to do so. More important, it helped remind Tommy to respect people in authority over him. Tommy is now a grown man, doing very well with a family of his own.

One of my greatest pleasures is to have young men like Tommy return to the Ranch, all grown up and married, with families in tow. Whenever one of their children says "Yes, sir" or "No, ma'am," a smile comes to my face. *Hmmm. I wonder how they learned that?*

Our children need to know that we love them, that we will always be truthful with them, and that we will always stick with them, through thick and thin. They also must know that when they violate the rules of the home, or the rules of society, there will be consequences for their actions and attitudes.

It will be frustrating for both you and your child, however, if you fail to inform your child of the boundaries in which you expect him to operate. In our next chapter, we will explore why boundaries are so important for your child, how you can set reasonable ones, and how you can help your child stay inside them. Before that, though, I have some questions that will help bring this chapter into focus for you.

THE WINNER'S FOCUS

1. How do your children know that you love them? What conditions do you sometimes attach to your love for your children? Do you say, "I love my daughter because

she is such a good girl." How would your love for her be impacted if she were not a good girl? Is your love for your child actually measured: "I love you if . . ." or "I love you because . . ." or "I love you in spite of . . ."?

2. Why is it important to always speak the truth to your children? What is the difference between "a little white lie" and an outright untruth? Remember, a broken promise is a lie to a child. Are there any broken promises you need to fix or make right?

3. What are some ways that you can assure your children that you will stick with them, no matter what? How would you have responded if you had been Tim Hansel's dad and Tim was your boy in trouble?

4. Can you forgive your children when they let you down? Is there a grudge in your heart against your children for something they have said or done? Our first response is "Absolutely not!" But in the past, have your children said or done something for which you have not forgiven them? If so, you have stifled the flow of your unconditional love for them.

5. Does your child know that there are boundaries in which their conduct and attitudes are acceptable? Why or why not? How can you help your children to understand that if those boundaries are crossed, severe consequences will be administered in response to the offense?

6. Respect is an honorable quality to teach our children. What are some ways you plan to help your children develop respect for the authorities under which they live?

7. What one area do you want to improve as a result of reading this chapter? How will positive changes in your actions or attitudes help to bring out the winner in your child?

4

Where Are the Boundaries?

*T*HE STADIUM WAS packed and the home-team crowd was cheering wildly as the clock ticked away the final seconds of the most important football game of the season. The visiting team was ahead by four points; a three-point field goal would not help. We had to score a touchdown, but our chances did not look good. We had the ball on our own twenty-yard line, with less than a minute to play.

Three times our quarterback attempted long passes, hoping a reception could get us down the field in a hurry. Three plays in a row the defensive backfield covered our receivers perfectly and thwarted our best efforts to score. We were down to our last chance, with only eight seconds showing on the scoreboard clock.

We needed a first down in order to stay alive and hopefully have another chance to complete a pass. The crowd noise was nearly deafening as the quarterback dumped off a quick screen pass to our tailback, who darted across the line of scrimmage, through a gap in the defensive line, and into the defensive backfield. The runner feinted sharply to his left, and then cut back to his right. The fake froze the defensive cornerback, and our runner ripped away from the pack of pursuing defenders. He crossed the line of scrimmage, and made the first down, then he picked up speed and raced across the next yard marker. He was still going!

Up the sideline he flew, with not a single opposing jersey standing between him and the goal line. Eighty yards he ran! One by one the defenders gave up trying to catch him and finally had to resign themselves to watching him dance across the goal line for a touchdown.

The crowd went wild! Thousands of people, including the fans, the players on the field, the coaches, and players along the sidelines, were cheering, waving our school colors, jumping up and down, and generally going nuts because the home team had scored the last-second touchdown. Time had run out on the clock. The game was over; we had won!

Suddenly a hush fell over the stadium, as every eye in the place focused on the forty-yard line. There, waving his arms, with his foot pointing at the white sideline, stood a referee. A collective gasp seemed to suck the air out of the home side of the stadium as the fans began to realize that the referee was indicating that the ball carrier had stepped out of bounds.

The touchdown was called back. Time had run out; the game was over. The runner had not scored, and we had not won the biggest ball game of the year. The ball carrier had crossed the line; he had stepped out of bounds. Subsequently, in a split second, our joy turned to frustration and sadness.

Anyone who has ever been a part of a sporting event, either as a participant or a spectator, knows the role of boundaries. The game must be played inside the lines.

Similarly, in life, our children have to run within the boundaries so that when they score, it will count; it will be right and they will win. They will finish the course successfully. It doesn't matter how much effort they expend, or how good they look, or even how loudly the crowd cheers. If our children do not operate within the boundaries, what they do will not count.

But how will your children be able to stay within the lines if you do not teach them where the lines are, or even that the lines exist?

WHY BOUNDARIES, ANYWAY?

Nowadays many parents need to know that it is okay to establish boundaries for their children. For several decades now, our society has emphasized the unfettered, unregimented freedom of children to do pretty much as they please. "Let the children call their own shots. We don't want to do anything to harm their creativity or freedom of expression."

We have swallowed this mush and an entire diet of psychobabble fed to us by television talk shows as though it was the greatest tasting stuff in the world. Like cotton candy, there's not much to it and a little bit does a lot of damage. As a result, we are now enduring a multitude of heartaches, headaches, and stomachaches.

Many contemporary parents have been reluctant to set boundaries for their children and even more have been hesitant to discipline their children when what few boundaries the parents have dared to establish have been crossed. Consequently, we have been raising self-centered children, with low tolerance for anything that requires work, sacrifice, or obeying the rules. Their inability to follow rules and get along with other people inevitably gets our children into trouble with their family members, peers, coworkers, or the law.

Ironically, the children we have been raising without firm boundaries are growing up with low self-esteem, a sense of incompetence, irresponsibility, and lack of confidence. Children who grow up with few boundaries may later interpret their parents' lack of restrictions as a lack of love, concern, and an indifference toward them.

It is time to turn this downward trend around, especially at home. Today is the day to begin setting boundaries for your children. Why wait until your children get into serious trouble in their personal relationships or with society's laws before you begin giving them some firm guidelines to help them down life's road? Every day you put off establishing boundaries, you will encounter more resistance and rebellion from your children when you eventually do try to draw some lines. The longer your children are unaccustomed to restraints, the more difficult it will be to apply them, and the more your children will buck against the boundaries once you have established them.

The main purpose of setting boundaries and clearly explaining them to your children is so everyone in the family knows what sort of conduct is expected. Of course, as a parent, you also establish boundaries for your children because you want to protect them, you want to keep your child safe, and you want them to know that you love them enough to set limits on what they can do. Setting realistic limits on your children's activities, vocabulary, and attitudes will not stifle their personalities. In many ways, limits are liberating for children and for you as the parent. Once they know where the boundaries are, they are free to operate comfortably and with extreme confidence within those limits. As the parent, setting limits and establishing boundaries help you to guide, direct, mold, and care for your children. The key to setting realistic boundaries is teaching your children what is expected of them rather than simply punishing them when they cross invisible or unclear lines.

The concept of setting boundaries for our children is neither new nor radical, yet multitudes of parents refuse to define limits for their children until it is too late. They then react with surprise and horror at their child's unsatisfactory or unacceptable behavior. At Big Oak Ranch, we get phone calls daily from well-intentioned parents who feel like throwing up their hands and quitting and many do. Often the cause of their frustration can be traced to their unwillingness to set boundaries. Consequently, the life of their child is spinning out of control. For the sake of your family, you cannot quit. You must not make that same mistake; you must establish and maintain boundaries for your child.

We deal with boundaries every day of our lives in dozens of practical, down-to-earth ways. Lines on the highways allow us to drive more rapidly and with less chance of bumping into someone else; fences, hedges, and trees line our property and say to some people, "Keep Out" and to others, "Come on in." Swimming pools have ropes that indicate where the deep water begins, a clear sign of danger to the person who cannot yet swim. Having tangible and easily understood boundaries lowers our stress level and helps us to enjoy safer, more productive, fulfilling lives.

According to Dr. Henry Cloud and Dr. John Townsend, codirectors of the renowned Minirth-Meier Clinic West:

> Boundaries are designed to keep the good in and the bad out. And skills such as saying no, telling the truth, and maintaining physical distance need to be developed in the family structure to allow the child to take on the responsibility of self-protection.[1]

In other words, by setting boundaries, you are helping your children learn to say yes to what is right, healthy, and good, and no to what is wrong, dangerous, or bad.

Your children especially need these boundaries in the formative years. For eighteen years, your children are like freshly poured concrete. If you do not have a firm form, the concrete is going to run all over the ground and all you are going to have is a globby mess. By the time the kids turn eighteen, you will have a hardened globby mess wherever you spilled the concrete. The concrete that runs onto the ground without a form will not be useful or productive, but the concrete set in a strong form will mold and solidify into the desired shape.

An interesting aspect of concrete is that it sets and cures in a matter of hours. While it is still wet, you can reshape it or redirect it again and again. Have you ever used your finger or a stick to sign your name in wet concrete? You can only rewrite or correct errors of judgment up to a point. After that, the concrete solidifies and your opportunity to make your mark upon it is gone. Similarly, you have only a short time to write your signature on your children's hearts and minds. The longer the wet concrete sets, the harder it gets, the more difficult and costly it is to change. Once it is completely hardened, or cured, the concrete is impossible to change without massive damage.

On the other hand, if you will build the forms the way you want that concrete to be molded, when your children turn eighteen, they will have a strong foundation upon which to build the rest of their lives and reproduce the same qualities in their own future children, your grandchildren.

BOUNDARIES NEED NOT BE RESTRICTIVE

When visitors come to Big Oak Ranch to see our program firsthand, they meet our staff, houseparents, and children. Often visitors are surprised that Big Oak Ranch maintains such a relaxed atmosphere. Children are laughing, playing, running, fishing, swimming, riding bikes, playing ball, building things, riding horses, camping in the woods, or doing a multitude of other "normal" things you and I may have done while growing up. Yet beneath the loose appearance is an extremely structured environment.

Our houseparents know where their children are—or are supposed to be—every minute of the day. The houseparents do not simply turn their children loose in the morning and hope they show up again at suppertime. For their part, the children know that they are responsible to keep their houseparents informed concerning any unexpected changes in the schedule. The children know that they have to check in with their houseparents throughout the day.

The most upset houseparent I have ever seen was upset not because of a flagrant act of disobedience in public. The most frustrated our houseparents become is when a child says something such as "I am going to the back pasture," but then actually wanders into the woods on the front side of the Ranch without letting the houseparent know where he or she is going. When the housedad goes to the back pasture looking for the child and discovers that the child is not there, the alarms go off. If the houseparents find that the child was not missing, but disobeying, that child is in big trouble!

Life is full of negative boundaries, but there are also positive boundaries. The negative boundaries are to protect. The positive boundaries are meant to mold your children into young people who can make wise decisions in the future. Not all boundaries are "No, no, no." Some boundaries are "Yes, yes, yes." Instead of constantly rebuking your children for doing things that are wrong, tell your children specifically what you expect. Rather than emphasizing conduct and attitudes that you do not want them to have, place the emphasis upon what you want.

For example, our daughter, Reagan, asked for and received permission from Tee and me to go to a movie at 9:00 P.M. She was fourteen years old at the time. When she and her friends arrived at the theater, they discovered that the movie they wanted to see did not begin until 9:45 P.M. Reagan didn't think much of the delay; after all, what is forty-five minutes when you are fourteen? She never thought to call home to tell Tee and me, "Mom, Dad, the movie starts at 9:45. I am going to be home a little later than I anticipated." Reagan just went on to the movie assuming it was going to be okay.

It wasn't okay.

When she came home forty-five minutes later than we had expected her, Tee and I met her at the door. We were not upset, but we were extremely firm. We asked, "Why didn't you call?"

Reagan was genuinely surprised at our concern. She replied, "I thought that since you knew I was at the nine o'clock movie, you would not worry about me. I never thought about calling at 9:45. I'm sorry to upset you, Mom and Dad. If something like that ever happens again, I will be sure to call."

Our stressing the fact that we expect her to call when she is going to be late was not negative or restrictive. It was a positive boundary in that it caused her to be accountable for her time, actions, and whereabouts, and it provided Tee and me the information we needed as parents concerned for her safety and whereabouts.

Today, if Reagan is faced with a similar set of circumstances, she simply calls home and says, "The movie starts at 9:45 so instead of getting out at 11:00, we will get out at about 11:45."

"Okay, fine. We will see you around midnight." End of discussion. But the positive boundary makes life better for everybody in our family.

BOUNDARIES MUST BE CLEAR AND SPECIFIC

Many people have asked me, "How do you handle so many children at Big Oak Ranch?" The answer is relatively simple: We have established clear and specific boundaries for our children. These boundaries include, but are not limited to, the physical boundaries of our property lines. They also include the moral, ethical, and attitudinal boundaries within which we expect our children to operate. If there were no clear boundaries, or the rules were hazy and fuzzy, we would be asking for constant conflicts stemming from unmet (and often unknown) expectations.

Children who live with unclear parental expectations will experience a sense of frustration, confusion, ineptness, unworthiness, and usually rebellion. Their response is not necessarily one of hostility, but more often one of ignorance. They simply do not know what conduct their parents consider acceptable. The boundaries are too vague.

Here are a few examples of loosely defined, nebulous boundaries:

- "Be a good little boy [or girl]."
- "Make sure you get home early."
- "Behave yourself."
- "Go put on some decent clothes."
- "Act your age."
- "Settle down."
- "You are watching too much television."

In setting boundaries for your child, you will both be much happier if you say specifically what you expect. For example, instead of saying, "You are watching too much television," you might say, "Tonight, you can choose one television program to watch, as long as it fits within our family values." Even here, however, you will have to adopt some guidelines about the content of the programs your children may watch. Whatever you allow or disallow, you must specifically decide what options are available to your children and then clearly inform them of their choices before they are given the opportunity to make their decisions.

Once when Brodie and I were watching television together, he had the remote control in his hand and was channel-surfing, looking for something we might enjoy watching together. We crossed a channel that was inappropriate. Brodie switched the channel without my having to say a word. Later, when I was in the kitchen, and Brodie did not know I was still watching the television, something else inappropriate came on the screen and Brodie switched the channel again. Why? Because he knew our family's standards about what type of programs we allow. He chose not to cross the boundaries because he knew the values of our family.

AVOID OVERDOING IT

The wise parent will set boundaries that are firm, yet still allow enough room for children to make choices within those boundaries. Rather than inundating them with a ton of rules about every little detail of their lives, you would be better off to establish hard-and-fast rules about those things that are truly important to you. You may tell your children, "You can play in our yard, but do not go out on the road." The yard becomes the boundary. You do not have to say, "You may play on the swings, play catch with a baseball, ride your bike on the driveway, play with your dolls on the picnic table, or play hopscotch on the patio." Allow your children to make choices within the framework of the larger boundary—the perimeter of the yard.

If a child crosses the line and goes out of the boundaries,

you must discipline him for his disobedience. We will examine various methods of discipline later in this book, but for now, understand that you cannot ignore a crossed boundary. If you want your child to play within the lines, there must be an appropriate penalty for going out of bounds.

Certainly, when establishing your children's boundaries, you must consider the children's ages and maturity levels. Not all children are able to do the same things at the same ages. For example, you may allow one child to date at sixteen years of age, but another of your children may not be ready to date until seventeen or even older. You must also consider what is socially acceptable for your child. Obviously, some behaviors are frowned upon in certain circles and accepted in others. Where I live in Alabama, it is considered quite acceptable to eat barbecued chicken by holding it with your fingers. In some other parts of the country, to eat chicken without a knife and fork would be considered uncouth. (Okay, I confess . . . you can call me uncouth!)

Parents have wide differences of opinion about what sort of conduct is age-appropriate and socially acceptable. Some parents can put up with almost any kind of conduct, as long as it is their child who is doing it. On the other hand, other parents have no tolerance for anything but the strictest standards of behavior from their children. Their children are expected to be perfect little angels, to be robots rather than children. Children are not little adults and should not be expected to be such. Somewhere between these two extremes of strictness and tolerance is an area in which you can wisely set realistic boundaries for your children.

In establishing boundaries, you should seek to maintain a balance between *fairness* and *firmness*. Let me explain. Imagine that you want to teach your children to drive a car down a narrow, one-lane road with a fence on each side of it. The fence on the one side is known as *fairness*; the fence on the other side is known as *firmness*. Before you give your children the keys, you explain a few things about the road they are about to travel. The trip will last a number of years, and the more successfully they drive, the wider the road will get. If your child does not negotiate the road well, or if they get off track, the road will become more narrow. As the parent, it is your job to adjust the controls that will widen or narrow the boundaries each day.

It is important that your child's boundaries and the corresponding penalties for crossing the boundaries are fair as well as firm. Once when Reagan was a toddler, I was having trouble trying to fit her feet into a new pair of shoes. I had just taken the shoes out of the box, so I was sure they were the correct size. Nevertheless, I could not squeeze her little feet into the shoes. Reagan would wiggle and wail every time I tried to insert her foot into one of the shoes. Like many dads, my attitude was, *If at first it doesn't work, use more force*. But the more I pushed Reagan's foot into the shoe, the more she cried.

I said, "Reagan, quit whining!" as I tried again to force her foot into the shoe. She yelped like a whipped puppy. I knew she was already feeling badly, not to mention the fact that her foot was taking a beating. But I chewed her out anyhow.

I decided I'd put my power into the next attempt. I picked up the shoe, stretched it with both of my hands as though I was doing isometric exercises. I turned the shoe upside down and as I did, something fell out of the shoe. It was a wad of paper stuffing that had been stashed in the front of the shoe to help maintain its shape. It would have been impossible to fit Reagan's foot into that shoe as long as that paper was in there, but I was so busy being firm with my daughter that I had not been fair. Besides that, I felt extremely foolish. I picked up Reagan and hugged her. I cried and told her that Daddy was sorry. I knew I had been too hard on her and for no real reason. I was trying to force her feet into boundaries that were too small, and therefore, unfair.

Even when your child deserves to be disciplined, you must always make sure you are fair in your reprimands. As an example, say your child crosses a boundary you have set about getting into the refrigerator between meals, and in doing so, he spills a container of milk. At that point, your child does not need a hard spanking. At that point, as psychologist and *Birth Order* author Kevin Leman is fond of saying, "We don't need a lecture; we don't need a sermon. What we need is a rag!"

On the other hand, if your ten-year-old son takes a knife and cuts holes into your furniture, you cannot simply shrug your shoulders and say, "Oh, well . . . boys will be boys!" Your child has crossed a boundary and you must respond with firm discipline. Unless, that is, you plan on having an entire room decorated with knife slices.

At Big Oak Ranch, we keep our boundaries flexible when necessary, firm when the children's actions so dictate, but we always work to be consistent. We do not allow our children to have one standard of conduct in public and a different one at home. You cannot have double standards when it comes to setting boundaries. You cannot allow children to act inappropriately at home and then punish them when they do the same things in public.

I learned this lesson the hard way with Brodie when he was five years old. I was allowing Brodie to use incorrect table manners at home, similar to those I had used at the athletic dorm while I was in college. I knew Brodie's actions were wrong, yet I rarely said a word to correct them. Once, when he was with me, out with a group of associates eating lunch at a restaurant, he ate in the same manner. I was extremely embarrassed about my son not using his fork correctly. Being the "expert parent" that I am, I jumped all over him about it. In front of the entire group, Brodie turned to me and innocently protested, "But, Dad, that's how we eat at home!"

The inconsistency was not his problem; it was mine. I was wrong for allowing two sets of standards to exist for Brodie. I jumped on him verbally, not because he was wrong, but because I was embarrassed. Regrettably, we parents often discipline out of embarrassment rather than for nobler reasons such as establishing boundaries. After that incident, Tee and I established new boundaries in acceptable table manners around the Croyle home. Since then, neither Brodie nor I have been similarly embarrassed in public or at home.

We maintain the same standards for the families at the Ranch. Not long ago, my family and I ate in a restaurant in which a housemom, housedad, and eight of our Ranch children had eaten the previous day. The owner of the restaurant came up to me and said, "We had some of your kids from the Ranch in here yesterday, and I want you to know I have never seen that many well-mannered kids in one place at one time."

Do I need to tell you how proud that made me feel? How would such a compliment make you feel? Mom and Dad, that restaurant owner did not notice our children's behavior because we are such great parents. It was because we have established realistic boundaries for our children, and our children have learned at home what is acceptable conduct in a public place. They have come to understand that some boundaries are inflexible.

INFLEXIBLE BOUNDARIES

Parents often ask me or other staff members at Big Oak Ranch, "What are inflexible boundaries?" Simply put, inflexible boundaries are the rules that do not bend, no matter what the circumstances.

We have a large number of animals at the ranch, and it is always interesting to watch the way our bulls learn to deal with boundaries. If a fence has a weak spot, or a wall has the least bit of give to it, that bull will keep nudging it with his shoulder, a little harder each time, until he is able to break through it. When that same bull encounters a hard, firm, inflexible wall or boundary, he backs off and stays in the pasture or stable where he belongs.

Similarly, when our children find a weak spot or a place where we are not as firm as we should be in our boundaries, they will keep pressing against that spot until they have gotten their way—if you allow them to do so. On the other hand, if they encounter a firm boundary, they may buck against it every so often, but they soon realize that life is much more enjoyable when they are not banging into rock-hard walls. Each family must decide what boundaries are inflexible, and then stick to them.

At Big Oak Ranch, for example, we will not tolerate drinking alcoholic beverages, using illegal drugs, smoking or using other tobacco products, or involvement in sexual behavior. Granted, we have had boys and girls who have stepped outside of every one of our inflexible boundaries. When that happens and we find out about it, the first thing we do is sit down with the violator. Together, we go through a step-by-step process of sorting out the facts. We deal specifically with these issues:

- Did you understand what you were doing?
- Did you know that what you were doing was wrong?
- Did you know what the consequences might be for doing such a thing?

We are equally as serious about other boundaries, not just blatant acts of rebellion. One of our boundaries is a Ranch curfew.

We are inflexible when we say, "Be home at twelve o'clock." If our children do not call when they know they are going to be late, regardless of the reason—a flat tire or a longer movie than they anticipated—our children get in big trouble with their houseparents. The children have been trained to understand that at twelve o'clock, if they are not home, the phone better be ringing to let us know where they are, and they better have a good reason why they are running late.

One time one of our seventeen-year-old boys had a car and a girl needed a ride home across town, which was twenty minutes out of the way. The boy knew he should call home before taking her home; he knew the boundaries concerning being home on time. He had been trained to call, but he didn't. He simply took the girl home, and although he knew he was running very late, he thought he could make it back to the ranch on time.

He successfully completed his mission of mercy. Unfortunately, in his attempt to beat the clock, on the way back from driving the girl home, he ran his car off the road. The boy escaped the accident unscathed, but he did about twelve hundred dollars' worth of damage to the car.

When his houseparents and I learned of the accident, our first concern was for his physical well-being. After we were certain he was not injured, I sat down with him and asked, "Were you where you were supposed to be?"

"No, sir," he replied sheepishly.

"Were you where you said you would be?" I pressed.

"No, sir."

"Did you call us to let us know that this girl needed a ride home and you were going to give her one?"

"No, sir."

"Should you have called us?"

"Yes, sir."

"Why didn't you call us?"

"Well, I didn't think you would let me take the girl home."

"Do you think if there was someone who needed a ride home and you had a chance to help that we wouldn't let you do it?"

"Well, no, sir."

"Well, then, young man, here is your discipline. You will pay for the twelve hundred dollars' worth of repairs to your car; you will pay it, in full, by yourself, with your own money. That is part one of your punishment. Part two, you will go straight to and from any meeting or school activity you need to attend, and there will be no turning left or turning right or giving anyone a ride home. You have lost that freedom because of your lack of communication."

If a young person makes a mistake once in this regard, we give him a warning. If he is late twice, then we say, "This has happened enough." The next infraction will result in greater restriction: He is not permitted to attend any social functions at night for a designated period of time. He has proven he is not ready to handle responsibly the freedom we have granted. When the time comes that we allow him to go out on his own again, we start from scratch. Usually, the child is much more time-conscious and the problem is solved. If not, we go through the process again, only this time the discipline becomes more stringent.

The key to all successful uses of boundaries is making sure that the boundaries are realistic and easily understood by the child.

In the next chapter, I am going to show you how easy it is to set specific boundaries. You may be amazed at how much more enjoyable life becomes for your child and for you once you have established realistic boundaries!

THE WINNER'S FOCUS

1. How do you define boundaries?
2. Why do you think many parents are reluctant to specifically establish boundaries and discuss them with their children?
3. In this chapter, we compared your child's formative years to freshly poured concrete. How dry is your child's "concrete"? What does this tell you?
4. Think of an area in which you have allowed hazy, unclear boundaries to exist for your child. How can you make those boundaries more specific?
5. List several areas in which you plan to establish inflexible boundaries for your child.

5

How to Set
Realistic Boundaries

WHEN ATTEMPTING TO ESTABLISH boundaries for your children, it will help if you mentally walk through a typical day in their lives. As you do, consider the options they might have during each segment of their day. Write down the choices you prefer and the choices that would be out of bounds. Be as specific as you can be. You won't have to do this every day, but like establishing and writing out a budget, it is worth the effort!

Start right at the beginning of your children's day. What are their boundaries in the area of getting up and getting ready for school, work, or play? Do you expect your children to make their beds, hang up their pajamas, or take a shower before coming to breakfast? Or do you prefer that your child wait until after eating to clean up?

How about eating breakfast? Is it okay for your children not to eat certain things? Or not to eat at all? Who cleans up the dishes after breakfast—the parents or the kids?

Going to school or work: Are your children allowed to travel to school with friends, or must they always go with you? What about school bus routines? Where do your children board the bus and where are they expected to get off the bus? What conduct is permissible aboard the bus? What about riding to or from school with friends who have access to automobiles?

Coming home from school: Do you expect your children to come straight home, or are stops along the way permissible? If stops are allowed, for how long?

As the parent, you should have answers to several questions before you allow your children to go anywhere without parental supervision, after school or otherwise: Where will they be? Who are they with? When will they be home, and how will they get there? Many parents who have allowed their children to take detours without having solid answers to these questions have experienced extreme heartache. Our newspapers, newscasts, and magazines are filled with reports of parents who paid the price of going to jail to bail out a wayward son or daughter, or worse still, were called to the hospital after their child was injured. The comment heard most often from parents when such tragedies occur is, "I did not know where my child was."

After-school activities: Sports. Music lessons. Practice sessions. When do they take place? For how long and under what circumstances? Are they conducted privately, out on the back porch, with friends, or with direct parental oversight? What are your rules for participating in other extracurricular activities? What are your standards about unchaperoned parties or trips? What are your standards concerning overnighters, pajama parties, and other things of that sort?

CHORES: YOUR CHILD'S OR YOURS?

What chores do you expect your children to do and when? Every child can do something to make life run more smoothly around your house—cleaning her bedroom, yard work, washing cars, kitchen and bathroom duties, running a vacuum cleaner, dusting furniture. Even small children can do something—folding towels, setting the table, helping to put clean dishes away. If your children are not accustomed to doing chores, try to make these fun activities for them and for you. You can make a race out of almost anything, not for competition, but for fun and for making special memories. As your children get older, the chores can increase in difficulty. These chores may not be as much fun, but they are still necessary and important. Chores for older children might include taking out the trash, raking leaves or shoveling snow, working in a vegetable or flower garden, or feeding and caring for pets.

All of our children at Big Oak Ranch have chores—no exceptions. We believe it is important that our children know how to work and work with a sense of pride and dignity. Larry Christenson, a highly regarded family counselor, believes the doing of chores—even mundane ones—is a key introduction to the discipline, sacrifice, and dedication necessary to doing a good job. Mr. Christenson writes:

> Nothing is so helpful in the training of a child as the opportunity for significant work. One of the real problems connected with the urbanization of our culture is that our children have fewer work opportunities. Nevertheless, parents must see to it that their children develop good work habits. Work around the home must be given over to the children as soon as they are able to handle it. The time which they have for play and leisure must be carefully proportioned

against meaningful, necessary work. Younger children spend proportionately more time at play. As a child grows older, an increasing proportion of time should be given to work. . . . "Work" in this sense also includes the responsibilities which a child has outside the home, e.g., school, school activities, sports, paper routes, baby-sitting, music lessons, and practice time. One of the simplest preventatives for juvenile delinquency is the building of good work habits. The great majority of delinquents have too much free time. They have not been required to shoulder genuine responsibility.[1]

Teenagers' chores may include mowing the lawn, vacuuming or mopping floors, or helping with grocery shopping. Chores should be tied to time limits to get them done. You may have a rule that beds must be made before breakfast. Yard work must be done before going to play. All chores should be done before any allowances are given.

BOUNDARIES FOR FREE TIME

What are your standards concerning part-time, after-school jobs for older children? What about playing with friends? Do you prefer your children always to play at your home or are they allowed to go to homes of friends? How are those decisions made? And who makes these decisions, you or your child? When you disagree, who wins?

CHILDREN ON-LINE

Watching television. How much time are your children allowed to spend watching television? What programs are permissible and what programs are off-limits? Do you have any standards regarding sexual content or the violent content of the programs you allow your children to watch? (You should!)

How will your children know if a program is off-limits? How do they know to change the channel when inappropriate material comes on the screen?

Another relatively new area that requires boundaries is your children's computer access time. Many of the concerns we have with television are intensified by access to the Internet. Similar to television, the computer can be a great tool in your children's education, but it can also open your children to a great deal of information they may not be ready to handle. Your children can now sit at computer terminals and tap into whole libraries of material you may consider inappropriate. Everything from child pornography to psychic experiences are readily available on the "information super-highway." As a parent, you must become familiar with what programs, games, CDs, and other material your children are accessing by means of a computer modem that is tapped into the World Wide Web.

Understandably, many parents feel inadequate because they are not as computer literate as their children, who have grown up with modern technology as a part of their lives. Nevertheless, you dare not ignore this area as you set boundaries for your kids. Multitudes of concerns involving computer use demand parental guidance and the establishing of boundaries.

In most cases, electronic lock-out devices—gadgets to block your children from accessing certain materials—will prove to be inadequate unless other boundaries are established concerning computer use. Although many of us parents have yet to figure out how to get the "12:00" to stop blinking on our videocassette recorders, our children have few problems with the new electronic wizardry. Rather than depending on technology to protect your children, a basic rule might be established to keep your child's computer in a public area of your home, not in your child's bedroom. At least then the screen is visible to all members of the family. Again, accountability helps. You are not a dictator, but simply the parent making a wise decision for the benefit of your child and your family.

BEDTIME, MONEY, MALLS, AND OTHER BOUNDARIES

After a busy day around your home, what is expected of your children at bedtime? Is there a standard time for them to go to bed? What activities are to be done before going to bed— baths, setting out clothes for the next day, reading time, family prayer time? How many times do you have to tell your kids it is time to go to bed?

Another area in which you should consider setting boundaries for your children's activities is the saving and spending of money. How do your children receive money? As gifts? Part-time jobs? Is their money put in a bank, or spent as the children please? What about allowances? Are they given with no strings, for no reason, or are they tied to certain responsibilities? It is best to make allowances contingent upon the completion of chores. Advances on allowances need to be limited to special extenuating circumstances. This allows your children to feel that they are contributing something of value and importance to the overall functioning of the family. Besides, your children's self-worth skyrockets when they start earning and saving their own money.

Are your children allowed to go to the mall with their friends? If so, when and for how long? Shopping malls have become the modern equivalent of the street corner of old, where both good and bad influences congregate.

What about your children's spiritual lives? Many of today's children hear God's name taken in vain far more than praised. What are you doing to counteract that? Do you require reading spiritual material? Is church attendance mandatory or optional at your house? Some parents say, "Well, I will wait until my child is old enough to decide for himself whether he wants to go to church." This is lofty idealism. Faith and values are important. Your children need them now and throughout their lives, not just after the majority of your parenting responsibilities are over. Besides, what better place than church is there to establish and reinforce standards of right and wrong? Certainly these values should be taught in the home. But if you take God out of your children's value system, on what absolute values are you going to base your standards of right and wrong?

DOES YOUR CHILD EAT WITH THAT MOUTH?

Do you allow your children to use profanity to express their feelings? What about slang? Language is always in flux. When I was growing up, *tough* meant "really cool"; *cool* meant . . . well, you know. In the recent past, however, we went through a period when bad meant that something was really great. The words are the same, but the meanings change with the times. Sadly, many words that were considered profane and repulsive as we were growing up have now moved into the mainstream of everyday language.

It is difficult for most parents to keep up with all the new slang terms children are hearing, bringing home, and using with their friends. Language trends come and go rapidly. Nevertheless, you should never allow speaking respectfully to one another to go out of style in your family.

When your children are with their friends, they may pop off, cut down, smart-mouth, shoot each other down with their words, rip on each other, crack back at each other, or otherwise use searing, biting, sarcastic remarks. Such talk just seems to go with the territory for many contemporary teenagers. But when your children come home and address their parents in the same way, it is wrong for parents to permit it. You and I, as parents, must establish a boundary that says such trashy talk will not be tolerated.

Smart parents I know remind or warn their children about boundaries and an impending confrontation if the children do not change their actions and attitude. Our children's language is one area where we may have to remind them even before they get to the boundary. For example, your daughter walks into your home after she has been with her friends, and she has a flippant attitude. She speaks sarcastically or disrespectfully to you or to others in the family. Right then, a wise parent will look at the child and say, "Now, Sally, I know you have been with your friends, and that sort of talk might be acceptable with them, but it is not going to work at home. I just want to make sure you don't cross that boundary line."

You have warned her before she broached the boundary. If you ignore the problem and allow your child to think that it is okay to use flippant or disrespectful language to family members, one day when you try to clamp down on her for being verbally abusive, you should not be surprised if you get no response. You should have warned the child long before you tried to nail her for some misdeed. Never fight a battle with your child that you do not have to fight, but don't be afraid to address an issue when necessary. Establish boundaries concerning your children's use of language before it becomes a problem by telling them, "I will not tolerate smarting off or speaking to me or other family members in a disrespectful manner." This might be done in the context of a discussion about manners or respect for teachers, ministers, and other elders.

Many of your children's attitudes toward you, their siblings, and their friends can be traced directly back to the words, attitudes, and facial expressions of a parent to his or her mate. I have heard husbands speak disrespectfully to their wives or vice versa. Later, when they have brought their child in for a counseling session, I have heard their child use the exact same words, attitudes, and facial expressions of the person who was using the disrespectful language toward his or her spouse. Many great family counselors have advised, "Mom and Dad, the best way to train your child to be respectful is to love your mate." (We can all do better at this.)

PICK A PLACE TO START

In each of the areas where boundaries are necessary, you probably have definite ideas concerning your preferences. Certainly, over a period of years, almost by osmosis and from your words, facial expressions, attitudes, and actions, your children will pick up on many of your likes and dislikes concerning their conduct. But wouldn't it save both of you a great deal of time and frustration simply to tell your children what you expect?

When communicating boundaries to your children, be sure to do it lovingly and with a positive attitude. You will probably have to repeat many of your standards—another good reason to write them down—so it is best to discuss only a few boundaries at a time. Avoid sounding like a dictatorial tyrant, but let your children know that certain types of conduct are acceptable, and others are not. When you are discussing boundaries with your children, use comments such as, "That is okay," or "That is not okay," "That is a possibility for you" or "That is not an option," "That is a choice" or "That isn't," and "This is acceptable" or "That is not acceptable." In other words, make clear which boundaries are firm and which boundaries allow the children a choice. Once you have stated what the boundary is—for example, "You are to be home by ten o'clock"—it is also a good idea to have your children restate the boundary back to you, making it personal: "I am to be home by ten o'clock." Not only will this clarify any confusion on your children's parts about what is expected, it will also help them to begin taking ownership of their boundaries.

Be prepared to explain why you want your children to do certain things. "Because I said so" might be a valid reason at times. More often than not, however, your children need to receive a better rationale behind the rule. If children get the impression that there is no real reason for the rule, it will not be long before they move toward thinking there is no real reason to obey the rule. This is especially important during the teenage years. In sports, the best head coaches I have seen inform their assistants and players so everyone knows what they are expected to do and why. Again, you do not always have to tell your children everything you know about a situation to explain the necessity for a boundary. But by letting your children know that their boundaries are not merely arbitrary, you will build their trust in your decisions.

THE FIRE HYDRANT THEORY

You cannot possibly start too early in setting boundaries for your children. For most of us, getting started too late, or getting started at all, is the problem. Regardless of whether you have allowed your child to live five, ten, or fifteen years with unspoken or unclear boundaries, it is imperative that you start. Granted, the older your children are when you begin to establish limitations and consequences upon their conduct, the more difficult it will be to get compliance with the new rules. The main issue is to get your children accustomed to living within boundaries. You may have to start by admitting your failure to clearly delineate the boundaries in the past. Then go on to say, "But there is a new sheriff in town, and starting today, we are going to live by a new set of rules." This must be an orchestrated, steady plan of action. You cannot impose a whole new lifestyle upon your child overnight.

Imagine that your child has been in the desert for fifteen years without water. Then suddenly you put him in front of a fire hydrant with a thimble. A zealous parent will unwittingly turn the fire hydrant on full blast in a misdirected attempt to make up for lost time. This is an error in judgment and timing. It also makes quite a mess!

Both you and your child will be better off if you start with a trickle to set new boundaries. Don't start with the big things, start with the small things. For instance, Billy's report is due on Monday. On Friday afternoon, you tell him, "We are not going to stay up all night to do your report on Sunday night. You can do it today, tomorrow, or after church on Sunday. But it must be done before Sunday night."

Gradually, as you and your child get your feet wet and become accustomed to the new way of doing things around your home, you can move from a trickle to a thimble to a cup, and finally to a bucket. Better to start slowly and work up to the changes you are making than to drown your child in a tidal wave of new standards.

Truth and Consequences

All the way along, let your children know that there will be consequences if they cross the boundary lines. The more specific you can be in spelling out the penalty for an infraction, the better likelihood of compliance. Avoid vague statements such as, "If you cross that line, you will be sorry," or "Be home by nine o'clock, or else!" Instead, place a specific penalty on breaking a specific boundary: "If you are not home by nine o'clock, you will be grounded for one week."

Be sure the penalty for crossing the boundary matches the circumstances. It is pointless to ground your child for one month because he dropped a glass of milk or pass off lightly your twelve-year-old when she defiantly challenges your leadership in the home.

Also be certain that you do not allow rules to replace your loving relationship with your children. As popular author and speaker Josh McDowell has often said, "Rules without relationship lead to rebellion." Focus on your relationship with your child, rather than the rules, and they will respond more positively to the rules. I know a dad who was gone an average of three and a half weeks per month and who would come home and spank his son harshly when a small rule was broken because the son has little respect for an absentee father. The dad had rules he wanted obeyed yet had no relationship with his son. The young son finally seriously rebelled, and the family is fragmented with little hope of recovery.

At all costs, do not ignore a broken boundary. Your children will not mysteriously wake up in the middle of the night and think, *I ought to stop doing that undesirable behavior I have been getting away with.* Dream on. You cannot ignore wrong behavior and simply hope it will go away. It won't. If anything, it will get worse. To ignore a broken boundary can eventually be lethal, not only to your boundary setting but to your child.

Neither should you spend endless hours arguing over or trying to explain the reasons for certain boundaries. Once you have provided your children with a basic understanding of why the boundary is important, and once they have a clear understanding of how they are to regard the boundary, continued negotiation will be damaging to your position as the parent. Certainly some explanations are necessary when you are establishing boundaries with your children, but no matter how well you explain some rules, they will not fully grasp the reasons— until they are parents! If you spend too much time trying to convince your children of the logical reasons why they should obey, it will only be a short time before somebody else convinces them of the logical reasons why they should disobey.

Similarly, overstated warnings, idle threats, and constant reminders of the boundary will soon fall upon deaf ears. Your child will simply tune out such vain repetitions. Only by following through on your promised disciplinary actions will you make your child realize that crossing a boundary is not an option.

This is not being a dictator; this is being a parent who is lovingly preparing your children for life. The key is respect. Because you are willing to set and maintain boundaries, at times your children may not like you, but they will respect you. Do you want to be liked by your children and disrespected, or respected by your children and loved?

COUNTDOWN TO INFINITY

Many parents use a countdown method to encourage a response from their children. "I'll give you to ten to get upstairs and get into bed!" "If you are not picking up your toys by the time I count to three . . ." Children have an uncanny way of knowing when your count is serious and when it is not. Often the countdowns get rather silly. Tom developed a countdown habit early in the life of Mark, his eight-year-old son. Tom yells out the back door, "Mark, I'll give you to three to get that bicycle put away and get in this house!

"One!"

No response.

"Two!"

No response from Mark.

"Two and a half!"

Still no action on Mark's part.

"Two and three-quarters!" Tom shouts loud enough for children in the next neighborhood to hear. Yet Mark continues ignoring the countdown.

"Two and seven-eighths!"

Mark knows very little about boundaries, but he does know his fractions quite well.

Other parents try to make their children obey through guilt: "You have it so rough, Mom. Life has been so unfair to you, so I guess I should obey you." Get real! Besides relinquishing your position as the parent, this sort of ploy forces your child into trying to compensate for your weaknesses. Don't do it, because you will reproduce a whiner instead of a winner!

Still other parents try to scare their children into obedience. They strike fear into the hearts of their children with wild stories about strangers stealing away with them if they don't hold Mama's hand, or the bogeyman will get them if they don't go to sleep, or the devil will mess them up if they go to that place, or some other fear-evoking idea. Rather than simply telling their children what conduct is acceptable, some parents try to prod the kids into obeying out of fear. It usually will not work for long, and even if it does, there will come a point when you probably will wish it hadn't. Do you want your child to fear the bogeyman or do you want your child to respect you?

Picture this: Your child is playing next to the curb on a busy street and you do not want her to get any closer to the street. You tell her to come back in. If she has no fear or chooses to blatantly disobey, she may go out into the street and possibly get hurt or killed. But if she has respect for you and your instructions, she will obey. A healthy fear can be lifesaving; it is far better that your child have this healthy fear of disobeying you than have a disregard for your requests and instructions.

The best way to inspire obedience to the rules is to clearly state the boundaries you expect your children to stay within and to specifically outline the consequences that will occur if they step out of bounds. Of course, the best boundaries will be useless if you are inconsistent or wishy-washy in following through on discipline when boundaries are broken—more about that in the next chapter.

BOUNDARIES WIDEN WITH AGE

You and I as parents establish the boundaries for our children, not the other way around. We widen the boundaries as our children's maturity, experience level, and ability to handle responsibilities increase, and not until then. Simply put, you can't have a sixteen-year-old living between a twelve-year-old's boundaries. By the same token, few twelve-year-olds can operate at a sixteen-year-old level. Certainly, there are exceptions to all rules. Some sixteen-year-olds behave like twelve-year-olds, in which case you must adjust that child's boundaries accordingly.

Sally, the sixteen-year-old, pitches a temper tantrum when you will not allow her to attend an unchaperoned party. She may be sixteen but she has just acted like a twelve-year-old. Treat her accordingly. If you usually allow your daughter to go out on Friday and Saturday evenings, take away a privilege: one of her nights out. When the emotions have subsided, explain but do not defend your decision. Let your daughter know that when she behaves like a twelve-year-old, her sixteen-year-old boundaries will tighten, and you will treat her as her behavior demands. She must understand that temper tantrums are inappropriate behavior. Why? Because later in life she will quickly discover that temper tantrums do not work effectively (or for long) in the college classroom, in the workplace, or in a marriage relationship. This is where sticking to your boundaries will teach her an invaluable lesson. Keep this in mind as a general rule of parenting: Misbehavior met by discomfort will lead to modified behavior.

Still, in most cases, we should be ready and willing to expand the horizons of our children's boundaries as they are able to handle increased responsibility. Let's say you have an emotionally and physically mature sixteen-year-old ready for a driver's license, and you are trying to force that child to live within the boundaries of a twelve-year-old in that you don't teach him to drive a car, possibly because you are not ready for your child to gain independence. I can make a prediction for you: You are heading for trouble, and when it comes, you will say, "How could this have happened?"

The answer will be looking at you in the mirror.

I know, because there have been times when I have been too strict and not allowed the boundaries to expand as one of our Ranch boys or girls grew up. It was a lot easier on us to keep them within ten-year-old boundaries when they were fourteen-year-olds. Recently we had a ten-year-old who wanted to play miniature golf every Friday night. His sixteen-year-old brother did not want to play miniature golf; he wanted to go out with his friends to a movie. Thinking they were being fair, the houseparents made the sixteen-year-old play miniature golf. Before long, every time the sixteen-year-old addressed the ten-year-old child, it was with an angry and frustration-filled tone of voice. What was once a very loving relationship had deteriorated into one of irritation. We realized our mistake, and we gradually turned on the "fire hydrant of freedom," allowing the sixteen-year-old to do age-appropriate activities. Now the ten-year-old is happy and the teenager is learning how to handle freedom responsibly.

It is not comfortable for you and me as parents to let our "babies" go. You can do it willingly, allowing the child to learn healthy patterns, or you can do it reluctantly, with rebellious actions straining or possibly ruining your relationship with your children.

Why not enlist your kids' help during this potentially explosive period in your lives? Explain that you are new at this and you need their help at releasing or expanding the boundaries. Your children will recognize that you are not trying to hold on to the reins of control too tightly, but for their sake, you do not want to release them too quickly.

For most parents, when our children turn eighteen and leave high school to go to college or out in the business world, it is difficult to see them go. But the question is: Are they not ready to go, or are we not ready to let them go? Or are they not ready to go because we have not done our job as parents to prepare them to go?

The opposite scenario is equally devastating. It is wrong to expose a twelve-year-old to eighteen-year-old situations simply because you want your child to be more mature and experienced. I know a woman who was so excited about her daughter becoming a teenager that she ignored setting any limitations on her daughter's dating practices. She pushed her daughter to go out with older boys when the girl was only thirteen. The mom encouraged her daughter to grow up too quickly.

In my dealings with thirteen hundred children, plus thousands of others in counseling situations, I have not met many thirteen-year-old girls who can correctly and safely handle a relationship with an eighteen-year-old young man. It doesn't take a lawyer to figure out what happened. In the mother's zeal to have her daughter grow up, she ended up with a grandchild. Upon learning that her daughter was pregnant, the mother's first question to her daughter was, "How could you?" It was the right question, but it was being asked of the wrong person.

Most of us would ask that mother, "How could you? How could you be so unconcerned about your child? How could you be so foolish? How could you be so selfish as to attempt to live out your own dreams through your child?" Yet every day, sometimes in blatant ways and sometimes in subtle ways, we can make similar mistakes if we try to force our children to grow up too fast, or if we push our children into situations they are not mature enough to handle. Our children will grow up fast enough. Let's not push them out the door until they are ready to go.

"YOU DON'T TRUST ME!"

There are many ways you can set boundaries by saying "Yes." Less popular with your child will be the ways you set boundaries by saying "No." It is not uncommon for our children to confuse our refusal to expand a boundary prematurely with a lack of trust in them. This is only natural. Tensions often mount when you refuse to allow your children to attend certain events or go out with a certain group. Your child may look at you and say, "You don't trust me."

Or perhaps you will hear the age-old question heard by parents of teenagers down through history: "Why are you treating me like a child?"

How should you respond to this or similar questions? First of all, tell the truth. Don't play games; explain to your child why you feel the way you do. Children can spot an insincere attitude almost immediately, so do not even attempt to camouflage your concerns.

At times you may look back at your child and say, "In a way you are right. I don't trust you yet, in that environment." Nobody rides a bicycle for the first time and then jumps directly into the Tour de France. Nobody learns to drive a car and immediately enters the Indy 500. It takes time, conditioning, and maturing to develop the skills necessary to perform at winning levels.

One of my favorite places to visit is a fudge shop in Gatlinburg, Tennessee. I could stand for hours, watching the fudge-maker inside a huge window, as he pours hot fudge onto a cool marble slate. He then takes a paddle and expertly works the mixture around the table, turning the creamy fudge over and over, adding ingredients, shaping it, patting it, knocking off any rough edges. All the while, the fudge-maker must be conscious of the temperature of the fudge as he is preparing it. If he allows it to cool too rapidly, the fudge will become brittle. It will be hard, and it will break into pieces easily. If he cools it too slowly, the fudge becomes sloppy and gooey. Neither the brittle nor the gooey is acceptable fudge.

So it is with your children. They may have all the necessary ingredients for greatness but become brittle if you push too fast; these children will be fragile and easily broken. On the other hand, if you allow your children to remain idle or to remain too long in one place in the growing-up process, they can become lazy, sloppy, and gooey. It takes a combination of timing, shaping, experience, wisdom, and asking God daily for discernment to bring out the winner in your child.

That is why when you know your children want to do something beyond their maturity level, you must lovingly look them square in the eye and say, "Trust has nothing to do with my answer. In my judgment, this is not a place you need to go. You are not ready to run that particular race."

For example, I would not have wanted my fifteen-year-old daughter going out with a group of college students. Not that I wouldn't trust my daughter or the college students, but the college students are not mine. I do not know how they were trained. They might say and do things that a fifteen-year-old child is not ready to experience, prepared to deal with, or fully able to understand. Think about it for a moment: Were you the same person at twenty-one years of age that you were at fifteen?

Let's take that just a little bit farther. Let's say you have a ten-year-old who doesn't know anything about the "birds and the bees" and he is going out with a bunch of fifteen-year-old, hormone-filled, girl-crazy boys who are trying to figure out what is going on with their bodies. They have nothing in common except sports. The ten-year-old's voice has not changed; his body has not matured. The fifteen-year-olds are almost fully developed young men. What do fifteen-year-old boys talk about? Sports, music, and girls, not necessarily in that order and absolutely not in equal proportions.

You have to be wise enough to realize that your child is not ready for this sort of influence. This does not mean you can choose your child's friends. It does mean you must use sound judgment when you know something or someone is not a good influence upon your child or that your child is not ready for that influence.

And don't feel badly about it! Restricting your children's activities does not reveal a lack of trust in your child. Trust has nothing to do with your decision. It is just sound judgment on your part to keep your children from situations they aren't ready for.

Even the Best Parents
Sometimes Make Mistakes

It takes a great deal of wisdom and discernment at this point to know when to expand, constrict, or maintain the boundaries we have set for our children. Even with wisdom and discernment, do not be discouraged if, at times, you make a wrong decision about your child's readiness to handle certain responsibilities. I have made mistakes in this area and have given some twelve-year-olds too many boundaries; others I have given too wide a berth in which to operate. At times we have held some children back from assuming responsibilities earlier in their lives because we were wrong in our discernment of the child's maturity level. Our motives were right, but our evaluations were wrong and so was our timing. Still, setting a slightly mistaken boundary for a child is better than setting no boundary at all. Ask yourself, Is my motive right, is my evaluation right, and is my timing right? More than likely, if all three can be answered affirmatively, you are on the right track in your understanding of the situation.

Effectively giving your children increased freedom and responsibility as they mature and are able to handle them is an important part of maintaining realistic boundaries. In his book *How to Keep Your Kids on Your Team*, Charles Stanley suggests:

> Your rules and limitations must be flexible. If your children are to become responsible adults who can function successfully outside your authority, it makes sense that certain limitations must be dropped or adjusted as they grow up. This does not mean you are compromising your convictions in any way. It simply means you are allowing them to decide some things for themselves. After growing up in your home, they should know how you feel about things. There comes a time, however, when they must be given the freedom to choose their own way, and it is better for them to be allowed to make those choices before they leave home.[2]

A frazzled mom approached me after I had spoken to her parent-teacher organization on the subject of boundaries. "I am deeply concerned," she began. "I am at my wits' end. My sixteen-year-old son has always stayed within the boundaries his father and I have established for him. He has always been a good boy and still is, but lately he has really been pressing on our boundaries, as if to see how far they will stretch before they break. What should his father and I do?"

I grinned at the woman and said, "Count on him pressing you. And be thankful."

I went on to explain that it is not only normal for teenagers to begin pressing at the boundaries, it is desirable. The more mature our children become, the more they begin to press on the boundary lines. They are trying to discover where the fences are firm and where they might have a bit more flexibility. Your child needs to know that some boundaries are meant to expand as the child matures and some boundaries will never move, regardless of the child's age.

In fact, if your teenage child does not occasionally test the boundaries, I would tend to worry. Another woman walked up to me at that same meeting and asked, "Can you help me with my son?"

"What's the problem?" I inquired.

"I can't do a thing with him. I can't get him up in the morning; I can't get him to go to school. I can't get him to help around the house; I can't get him to clean up his room; I can't get him to mow the yard . . ."

I had the feeling that the woman's list could go on and on, so I gently interrupted her by asking, "Well, ma'am, how old is your son?"

"Twenty-three," she replied.

That woman had a problem! Not only should she have applied some accurately placed foot action to her son's backside, the young man himself should have been bucking at the door trying to get out into the world and do something with his life! Seriously, that woman should have been leading her son out the door. It was time—no, it was past time. She was nearing the point of no return, when it would be too late to make any effective adjustments in her son's game plan for life.

If you have a seventeen-year-old son, that young buck

should be pawing at the ground and pressing against the door, anticipating the time when he can get out on his own. It is not abnormal; it is healthy. It means he is growing up; his engine is working on all cylinders. It does not mean that you drop all the boundaries you have been holding in place all these years. It merely means that you realize that your parenting job is drawing to a close. Your child is almost ready to go off to college, into the workplace, into the military, or some other option, and you have worked yourself right out of a job. This is exactly how parenting is supposed to work!

MAINTAIN A UNITED FRONT

One other suggestion concerning the setting and maintaining of your children's boundaries: As in any aspect of parenting, all adult family members must present a united front. You cannot expect your children to comply with the boundaries you have set, if you, your spouse, or your children's grandparents are constantly ignoring the known, established boundaries. Grandparents, of course, are notorious for being lenient with their grandchildren. But if they consistently disregard the lines you have set, you will have to confront them in a loving manner. Let them know that if they really want to help you do the best job of bringing out the winner in your children, Grandma and Grandpa will have to play by your rules too! Grandma and Grandpa had their shot at parenting; now it is your turn. Of course, whether your child's grandparents were great parents or poor parents, you can learn from them. But never forget, your children are *your* responsibility; you must raise them according to the standards you have set.

Most important of all, Mom and Dad must maintain a united front concerning boundaries and the consequences for crossing them. Never allow your children to play one parent against the other.

Twelve-year-old Joey wants to go swimming. Several of his buddies are going, and he explains that to Mom, but she still says, "No, you can't go swimming."

Later that afternoon, when Joey's dad gets home from work, Joey, playing the system, goes to him and asks, "Dad, can I go swimming?"

Unaware of Joey's previous conversation, his dad says, "Sure, I'll run you over to the pool."

Joey has just played the two ends against the middle. When he could not get what he wanted from one parent, he went to the other and succeeded in getting his way. How do you handle a child who is playing two ends against the middle?

First and foremost, Mom and Dad must maintain a united front. To do so, you must engage in open communication about what is going on in the lives of your children. You cannot assume that you know what your marriage partner would say about a particular situation concerning your child. You must talk about it.

When a child attempts to pit one parent against the other, you must sit down with the child and say, "Now, Joey, you asked your mom earlier today if you could go swimming. She told you no. When I got home, you asked me if you could go swimming, and I said sure. I didn't know that Mom had already given you a firm answer when I said I would drive you to the pool. Then your mom told me about your previous conversation.

"What you did was wrong, and because you did that, we are going to discipline you in this way."

Then you name whatever the punishment might be, whether it be grounding, taking away a privilege, or no swimming with his buddies for two weeks.

More important, you have reinforced the boundaries and explained to him that he cannot play two ends against the middle. You have demonstrated that you and your mate will talk, and when you find out he has attempted to play the two parents against each other or he has misrepresented the truth because he didn't give you all the facts, there will be negative consequences.

EXPECT OBEDIENCE, BUT BE PATIENT

Once the boundaries are established, if your children overstep those boundaries in blatant, rebellious ways, you must make the consequences of disobedience so unpleasant that they will think twice before casually violating the boundaries again. *Fair, loving, consistent discipline is the key to maintaining realistic boundaries.* If you fail to make your children wish they had not done the wrong behavior, you are inviting a repeat performance. Furthermore, if you fail to make your children understand the increasingly high cost of wrong behavior, they are unlikely to change it because there is no motivation to do so. Only when crossing the boundaries becomes a problem for your children will they avoid breaking the rules and operate comfortably within the lines.

Learning to stay within the lines does not always happen the first time a child steps out of bounds and experiences the consequences. Referees in a football game do not throw one penalty flag and then go sit down for the remainder of the game. Quite the contrary, when a player has committed a foul, the referee watches even more closely to make sure the same offense is not repeated.

As a parent, you will repeatedly have to make your children get back inside the lines, until it becomes a habit for them to stay on the right road. Don't be afraid to repeat disciplines, perhaps increasing the consequences, if your child continues to step out of bounds after being penalized. Take away more privileges or do whatever you must to train them that stepping out of boundaries is not the thing to do.

But how does a parent know what discipline is appropriate nowadays? Is it really possible to make your children mind without losing yours? You may be surprised at some of your discoveries in the next chapter.

THE WINNER'S FOCUS

1. Who sets the boundaries in your home?
2. List at least three areas in which you plan to set specific boundaries for your children. Begin by going through your children's day, from getting out of bed until bedtime that night. What areas need immediate attention?
3. You could probably do most of your children's chores quicker, better, and more efficiently. What value then do chores provide for your children?
4. What steps are you taking to ensure that your children are receiving a solid spiritual and moral base from which to decide issues of right and wrong? What changes do you need to make in this area?
5. To what extent do you allow grandparents to influence your decisions about what boundaries will be set for their grandchildren? In regard to grandparents, in-laws, and other relatives, learn from them, but do not be led by them. Listen to your relatives who are trying to help, and love them for their concern. Always remember, though, that you are responsible to train and manage your children. In what ways will you raise your children differently from the way in which your parents raised you?
6. Why is "Because I said so!" usually an insufficient reason for a boundary?

7. Describe the difference between love and respect.
8. How do you handle it when your child tries to play two ends against the middle in your home? On a scale of one to ten, ten being excellent, how well do you and your mate discuss the two ends your child is attempting to play against each other? On the same scale, how well do you jointly set boundaries and discipline when there is an offense? Remember, if you don't set the boundaries, somebody else will.

6

Children Want Discipline—Really!

MICHAEL WAS A TOUGH little boy. By the time he was twelve years of age, his mom and dad were both dead and he had been passed from home to home, living with a variety of foster parents. In the process, he developed some strong, antiauthority attitudes. He wasn't really a bad boy, but he could be mean, stubborn, and strong-willed over the smallest issue. Michael was a handful, to say the least. He came to live with us in the early years of Big Oak Ranch, when we were just getting started. I was not much more than twenty-five years of age myself and I was struggling in my efforts to find a balance between trying to help Michael feel loved and accepted, while at the same time making him follow our instructions. We both were learning about life.

One day Michael and I were standing in front of the porch of our farmhouse, and he was rubbing his toe across one of the pretty little roses growing in the yard. I said, "Now, Michael, don't step on those flowers. If you do, I will have to spank your bottom."

Michael looked up at me and then looked back down at the flower. A big grin slowly crept across his face. Without saying a word, he deliberately raised his foot as high as he could get it, then stomped on the flower with all of his might. As if to drive home his point, he took his foot and slowly ground the crushed flower into the dirt.

Michael looked up and smiled. He didn't say anything, but his look said, *What are you gonna do now, big boy?* You have probably seen a similar look from your child.

I was relatively new at this parenting thing, but I recognized a challenge when I saw one. I understood that Michael was testing me to see if I would keep my word. More important, although I did not realize it just then, he was testing me to see whether I really loved him.

I looked back at the little boy and I said, "Now what did I tell you that I was going to do if you stomped those flowers?"

The boy looked up and said, "You told me you were going to spank me."

I said, "Okay, come on inside."

Michael and I went inside the farmhouse, where I found a little Ping-Pong paddle, and I gave him three swats on his bottom for stomping on the flowers.

Michael did not shed a tear. He showed no sign of remorse. He simply looked at me and said, "You done?"

I interpreted Michael's matter-of-fact response as his way of saying, "Good, see there, I've taken your best shot, and it doesn't affect me."

I answered, "Yeah, but why did you deliberately stomp those flowers?"

"Because I didn't think you'd spank me."

"Really?"

His answer was in his eyes. They were saying, *No one has loved me enough to keep their word and discipline me.*

Although Michael's way of expressing it may be different from your child's, believe it or not, Mom or Dad, children want discipline—really! And parents who truly love their children will discipline them. Love without discipline is nothing more than sweet, syrupy sentiment that will eventually cause life to become real sticky for both you and your child. On the other hand, discipline without love can quickly become overbearing and dictatorial. Love and discipline are two sides of the same coin; the two must go together. You might say that discipline shows your children that you love them. And our children recognize the real thing when they see it. They also recognize the need for the real thing when they don't see it.

One day a young boy and his dad were in a grocery store. A woman and her little boy were in front of them in the checkout line. While they were all waiting in line, the woman's son reached out and grabbed something off the counter.

"Don't do that," the woman said sternly. For a few moments the boy obeyed, but soon he reached and grabbed the item on the counter again.

More emphatically, the woman said, "Now, don't do that or Mommy will spank." Within a few seconds, the boy repeated his actions. Again the mother issued her warning, "I told you if you did that again I was going to spank."

About the fourth or fifth time the woman threatened to spank the boy, the young boy looked up at his dad and said, "I sure wish she would go ahead and do it!"

Loving discipline gives children a sense of security. They know where the boundaries are; they know where the fences are and how far they can safely go; they know you love them because you are willing to discipline them.

Let me give you an example: Let's say your little girl is six years old, and she is riding her bicycle up and down the sidewalk in front of your house. You tell her, "Do not go past the corner. If you go past the corner, you will park your bike for the rest of the day." From previous experience, you have already established this boundary, and you are simply reminding her of the boundary and the consequence that have been set. But the next time you look up, sure enough, there she goes, right around the corner. Not only does she go around the corner, she goes all the way around the block!

When your daughter gets back from her round-the-block trip, you are sitting on the front porch, waiting. Now, what are you going to do, Mom and Dad? You told your girl what would happen if she crossed that boundary. Are you going to sit there and say, "I know I told you that you would have to park your bike if you went past the corner, but I will let you get away with it this time. Just don't do it again"?

Such a response may be appropriate on rare occasions, but if you continually compromise and neglect disciplining your child when she crosses established boundaries, you will create an intense insecurity within her. You are leading her to think, *Mom or Dad doesn't love me enough to keep me within those boundaries.* While you think you are expressing your love to the child by allowing her to do something beyond her boundaries, the child's perception of your lax discipline is just the opposite.

Interestingly, the Bible never commands our children to love us. The Bible commands children to honor us. But children will not honor what they do not respect. Many children love their parents, but they do not respect them. On the other hand, the by-product of being honored by your children is being respected and loved. Do you want to be honored, respected, and loved, or do you want to be loved but not respected? The value you place upon discipline will determine the attitude your children will have toward you.

Almost every day I have a parent call me and say, "I know my child loves me, but he doesn't respect me and he won't obey me." This parent made the wrong choice. He wanted to be liked, rather than honored by his child. You cannot be your children's best friend as they are growing up and forget you must be the parent too. Later in life, when your children are on their own, you and they may be best friends. That's great. But right now, your children do not need an adult friend; they need parents who will hold them within their boundaries and who will dare to discipline them when they step outside those boundaries.

The Difference Between Punishment and Discipline

Before we go any farther in our discussion of discipline, we need to define terms. Punishment and discipline are not the same. Simply put, punishment is negative and usually will bring about negative results in the lives of your children; punishment rarely builds anything but resentment. Discipline, however, is positive and will produce life lessons that will result in character traits such as responsibility, accountability, thoughtfulness, and obedience. Not coincidentally, these are the same qualities that your children can learn from and draw upon throughout their lives. While discipline may involve some elements of punishment, punishment alone is not discipline.

Punishment is often simply a parent's way of venting her own anger at something the child has said or done. It may momentarily relieve a bit of pent-up frustration for the parent, but it does very little to reinforce long-term positive actions or attitudes on the part of the child. Punishment merely inflicts some sort of pain—whether emotional, physical, or social—as a consequence of a person's misdeeds. Discipline, on the other hand, is a way of training your child to do the right thing.

My dad understood the difference between punishment and discipline. Dad made a promise to me when I was a boy: "I'll never spank you when I am angry." And he never did. Several times, however, he told me, "I'm so angry right now I can't discipline you." Oh, he spanked me, all right! But only when he was in complete control of his own emotions. When my dad disciplined me, it was always with an attitude, "What lesson can we learn from this?" He never administered discipline to me in a spirit of anger. Instead, his discipline always included a sense of what was wrong. Sure, he made some mistakes in his disciplining, but I knew where I stood with my dad.

Rather than administering discipline to your child when you are angry, say to the child, "Go to your room for a while and let's take some time to get control of our emotions. Then we will talk again. I will be in to see you in a little while."

Take a breather. Go sit down and talk with your mate about the situation. If your mate is not available or if you are a single parent, talk to a friend, or simply go someplace where you can cool down and honestly evaluate, *Now, why am I so angry?*

Are you angry because your child lied to you? Are you angry because he did something that violated your trust? Are you angry because your child crossed the boundaries? It is important to determine the reason behind your anger and to deal with it first. If you attempt to discipline your child out of your own anger, both of you will lose, because the child will not see the discipline; he will only see the anger. He will interpret your anger as directed toward him, not what he did. Beyond that, if you attempt to discipline your child out of your wrath, you will most likely cross the line and slip into punishment, maybe even abuse, rather than discipline. Always discipline your child out of your love, not your anger.

Think of it this way: Punishment is what we do to criminals when we put them in prison for life, or perhaps even inflict the death penalty. It is society's retribution toward the criminals for what they have done. Discipline, however, may put criminals in prison, but while they are serving their time, they are also learning what causes them to respond to life in negative ways, proper ways to deal with situations, and realistic adult boundaries. They may also be learning a skill they can use to productively contribute to society and perhaps pay back those they have hurt once they get out of prison.

Just as it is possible to discipline without ever physically touching your child, it is also possible to punish or even abuse your child without ever touching her. Often it is the spirit with which corrective measures are administered that makes all the difference. Be careful here! Your attitude will override your actions every time.

One of my worst weaknesses is that I tend to use my eyes to get my point across. All I need to do is to give my children or one of the Ranch children "the look," and they know they have crossed the line. But if all I have done is shown them my displeasure or anger over their actions, "the look" may be a form of punishment and I have not disciplined the child. Also, "the look" will lose its effect over time.

Sadly, many children cannot remember a time when their parents said, "I love you." All they ever got from their moms and dads were spankings, ugly looks, or attitudes that caused deep-seated, negative feelings. That is punishment rather than discipline.

Discipline Can Teach Quietly

On the other hand, it is possible to discipline our children without lashing out at them with angry words, actions, or glaring looks. As I was growing up, my mom and dad always told me, "Everything in this house is yours." I knew Mom and Dad both worked hard, and they bought and paid for our possessions. I also understood I was a valuable member of the family and everything belonged to me too. One item, however, held a special place in my mom's heart. It was an antique lead crystal bowl so prized because of its beauty and age.

One summer, a bunch of my buddies and I built a camp, sort of a makeshift clubhouse, in my back yard. It wasn't fancy, but to us it was the neatest camp in the world. It had a top, sides, and windows made out of tree limbs. We loved to crawl into our campsite and have fun. One day, about four of us had just gotten some pecans from some friends of ours in Southside, a little town near where Big Oak Ranch is now located. I ran into the house and retrieved some pecan-crackers from Mom's kitchen drawers. These were nutcrackers made like small metal visegrips with which pressure was applied to the pecans so they would crack wide open. I also brought out Mom's special antique bowl to put the shelled nuts in.

You can probably guess what happened. We were out there in our camp, eating pecans and having a great time. Suddenly, one of the guys dropped a nutcracker down into Mom's favorite bowl. The weight of the metal landed full against the fragile glass. Mom's prized possession shattered, glass and pecans mixing on the grass floor of our campsite.

When I finally worked up the courage to show the broken bowl to my mom, her reaction surprised me. She did not rant or rave about the lost bowl. She did not lose her temper or spew a litany of ferocious words in my direction. She did not even ask me why I had been so foolish as to use her special bowl while playing outside. She just looked at me and said, "I wish you hadn't broken it. I'm sorry you did, but your daddy and I have always told you that everything in our home belongs to you, as well as to us. It was your bowl too."

Mom did not punish me, but she sure did discipline me with those words. I never forgot that look of disappointment on her face, and I never wanted to cause her such pain again.

Mom got my attention without touching me. To some people, this may sound like *Leave It to Beaver*, but let me assure you it wasn't. My mom knew what pressure to apply in all the right places and for what period of time. She had great discernment in regard to boundaries and discipline, and she knew that sometimes restraint was more powerful than reproof.

WHEN RESTRAINT IS DISCIPLINE ENOUGH

Another time when I was a young boy, my mom was scheduled to host a women's meeting at our home. More than a dozen women were coming to our house for a party that night, and Mom had baked a beautiful cake and was letting it cool on the stove's cooling racks. The cake was a masterpiece—one of those special layer cakes that only mamas can make. When I came by the kitchen and saw that thing on the stove, I thought I was in heaven! I ran over to the cake and literally grabbed a handful of cake out of one of the layers. I didn't know, you see, that the cake was reserved for our guests. She was wise enough not to spank me or lecture me over the cake. She did, however, emphatically explain that the next time I saw a cake on the cooling racks, I should realize it was there for a reason and not touch it before checking with her. My mom's restraint in applying discipline has been a good example for me, one I have draw upon many times in deciding when and how to discipline my own children.

For example, one of my favorite possessions in the world is my blue, 1985 Jeep CJ-7. That vehicle is my toy. Everyone in my family refers to it as Daddy's Jeep. A friend of mine in Gadsden, who manages a car dealership, had it painted and striped for me, and it looks so good!

When Brodie was eleven years old, he and I were mowing my father-in-law's lawn. A plastic gas can containing extra gasoline was sitting on the ground near my Jeep, which was parked on the concrete driveway. When it came time to refill the mower's fuel tank, Brodie wanted to do his part to help. He picked up the gas can, set it on top of my Jeep's hood, and before I had a chance to say a word, he pushed it across the hood, toward where I was standing on the other side of the vehicle. The grating sound of that gas can scraping across my Jeep's hood is indelibly impressed upon my mind.

All across the Jeep's hood there was a deep scratch in the paint. As I looked at it, my horrified expression must have spoken a million words. Brodie looked at the scratch, took one look at me, and immediately cried out, "Daddy, I was just trying to help! I'm sorry."

I looked at my boy and I looked back at the scratched hood. I took a deep breath and said, "You know, buddy, nothing in this world is more important to me than you are. You made a mistake and, yes, this is my favorite Jeep, but you are my bud. You are much more important than any Jeep. The next time, please don't put the gas can on top of the hood of any car, not just Daddy's Jeep."

I didn't spank him. I didn't make him rub out the scratches or pay for the hood to be repainted. He knew the moment that he saw my face that he had done wrong. That was discipline without punishment because my son learned a lesson. I doubt that he will ever again put a gas can on the hood of any car. To me, that was all the discipline necessary, and it worked.

What is discipline? It is teaching and training our children in the right way to do things.

Before You Discipline

Certainly there are times for more direct forms of discipline. I will deal with specific methods of discipline later in this book. Before you administer discipline, however, you must first determine what you are going to do when specific boundaries have been crossed and what, if any, consequences for crossing those boundaries have been previously set.

When one of our children at Big Oak Ranch or in our own home says or does something wrong, something that crosses a boundary, the child's houseparents and I usually ask these three questions of the child:

1. Did you understand what you were doing?
2. Did you know that what you were doing was wrong?
3. Did you know what the consequences might be for doing such a thing?

If the child answers yes to these questions, we have established: (1) the child knew what she was doing; (2) she willfully disobeyed; and (3) she knew at the time she willfully disobeyed that crossing this boundary would bring unpleasant consequences. Children often get involved in things they do not understand are wrong or dangerous. Those types of infractions must be dealt with differently from incidents of willful disobedience.

Once it is determined that we are dealing with willful, rebellious disobedience rather than an accident or a mistake, we then have to determine through wisdom and experience what the most effective form of discipline is for this incident. As I mentioned previously, every child is different, and what works positively with one child may not be effective with another. Similarly, the discipline must be appropriate to the offense. It would be ridiculous to give your child four swats with a paddle because he forgot to tie his shoes. On the other hand, if your twelve-year-old takes your car and goes joyriding and you just pass it off as, "Oh, kids will be kids," don't be surprised when that child thinks that it is okay to steal somebody's car and go joyriding.

Do not allow too much time to pass between the offense and the discipline. Otherwise, the issues and the reasons for the discipline will become blurred in the mind of the child (and possibly in yours too). When you have decided what discipline is appropriate to your child's behavior, and how that discipline will help modify her behavior in a positive way while she learns a lesson, then apply it.

Afterward, look that child square in the eyes and say, "I love you. You have disappointed me, but I still love you and that hasn't changed. I do not want to have to go through this again, do you? Let's learn from this experience and go on." Then hug her.

Granted, she may not want you to hug her just then, but this is an important part of discipline. I strongly suggest that you do not ignore the immense value of this simple gesture of hugging your child after you have applied discipline. A hug is a way of sealing your relationship with your child. The hug closes the issue. It says, "Although I am not happy with your actions, it does not alter the way I feel about you." That is one of the keys to loving discipline.

On the other hand, punishment leaves a child with the idea, "My mom is not happy with what I did; therefore, she doesn't like me." Discipline should leave your child with the assurance that she is always loved, no matter what.

All of us want to be liked; all of us want to be loved—

especially by our children. Sometimes these desires cause us to be afraid to discipline, but discipline will help bring out the winner in your child. In the next chapter we will address fears about discipline and discover how we can overcome them.

THE WINNER'S FOCUS

1. How would you describe the difference between punishment and discipline? Think of a time when you wanted to discipline your child but actually punished him or her. Now that you have read this chapter, what would you do differently if a similar situation occurred?

2. Why is it important to get control of your own emotions before you attempt to discipline your child?

3. What effect does hugging your child have after you have disciplined him or her? Why is this closure so important in discipline and in the overall attitude of your child?

4. How would you explain to your child the relationship between love and discipline?

5. What discipline that you received as a child do you remember as being most effective in training you?

6. What discipline or punishment did you receive as a child that had no effect on you or caused a negative reaction in your heart? Have you ever disciplined or punished your child in a similar nonproductive way simply because it was how your parents disciplined or punished you?

7. Why will a lack of consistent discipline cause insecurity in your child?

8. Many parents delight in saying, "I am my child's best friend!" What, if anything, is wrong with that? What is the balance between being a friend to your child and being your child's parent?

7

Why Are We Afraid to Discipline Our Children?

*I*F DISCIPLINE IS such a positive experience for our children, why then are so many parents reluctant to discipline their children?

Usually it is because we are afraid our children will not love us if we do. As strange as it may seem, we are afraid our children will reject us. Some parents are also concerned that their children will be afraid of them as a result of discipline. Nothing could be farther from the truth. A child knows you love him because you discipline him. Certainly, he may dislike you at the time discipline is being applied. Do not let that deter you. You are training a winner. You must do your job!

At times when Brodie was a little boy and I had spanked him, my son turned around with tears and said to me, "I hate you!"

At that moment, he was probably expressing his true feelings. Nevertheless, I held him and. lovingly said, "I understand, buddy. I understand. I know right now you probably do hate me. But someday you will understand that the reason I must discipline you is because I love you so much."

Ten minutes later, my little boy would come up to me and say, "Daddy, I'm sorry for what I said. I shouldn't have said that. I don't hate you." He would fall asleep in my arms that night.

Children will not hate you—at least not for long—when you discipline them. They will not reject you. Your children might hate you or resent you if you do not discipline them, or if you try to pass off punishment as discipline. But if you discipline them correctly, they will love you, because they know you are teaching them the right way, that you are preparing them for the game of life.

The late Vince Lombardi is generally regarded as one of the greatest football coaches, and more important, one of the most effective motivators the sport has ever known. Interestingly, many of Lombardi's players hated him for making them do ten minutes of difficult, tedious grass drills every day when most other teams in professional football were doing only three minutes of the despised drills. When it came time for the big challenge on game day, however, Vince Lombardi knew his players were ready. More important, the players knew they were ready because they had paid a higher price to get there. The discipline they had endured was not fun at the time, but it paid huge dividends to the players in the long run. Most discipline is unpleasant for the teacher and the student, but it is part of training a winner.

In my life, Coach Bryant of Alabama had a similar influence on me. Every day Coach Bryant would look at his players before practice and say, "Gentlemen, let's get a little bit better today than we were yesterday. I don't want you to get a lot better, just

a little bit better. Every day let's get a little bit better." That is
the role discipline plays in our parent-child relationships; we
are helping our children to get a little bit better each day.

One of the keys to discipline is to get off your children's
backs and get on their team. I saw this powerfully illustrated
during the 1992 Summer Olympics. In the 440 meter race,
just as Derrick Redmond, a sprinter from Great Britain, was
making the final turn, he blew out his hamstring. His leg
buckled beneath him, and the sprinter fell to the ground in
pain. With a great deal of difficulty, but with sheer determination, he got back up and tried to limp toward the finish line.
The young man's dad saw his son go down, so he came out of
the stands to help. As the other runners passed him by, the
young man looked at his dad and said, "I have to finish."

His dad replied, "I am with you all the way." The dad put
his arm around his boy's waist and helped him limp the final
hundred meters.

Don't be afraid to train your child to run that 440 meters,
but don't let that be the only lesson. Another part of parental
discipline is knowing when it is time for you as a parent to put
your loving arms around your children, and give them a lift.
One day our children will do that with their own children. We
discipline our children now to help them to be disciplined
themselves, and to teach them how to be disciplinarians when
they have children of their own. If you are afraid to discipline
your child, you will cause your child to one day be reluctant
to discipline his children. On the other hand, if you model
loving discipline toward your child, that too will be passed on
to his children.

EXPERIENCE IS NOT THE BEST TEACHER
Most of us have heard the maxim, "Experience is the best
teacher." In many ways that is true. When it comes to spiritual

or philosophical debates, a man with an experience is never at the mercy of a man with an argument. When it comes to raising our children, however, in many ways, experience is a terrible teacher. It gives the test first; then you learn the valuable lesson.

If your teenager drives a car ninety miles per hour, he may experience the exhilaration of driving at excessively high speeds, but he may also have the experience of losing control of a car, rolling it, destroying the auto, and severely injuring himself or his best friends. Yes, your child will learn from the experience, but at what a cost!

The greatest teacher is not experience; it is *example.*

To me, the greatest example ever to walk the earth was Jesus Christ. If you want an adventure, read the four Gospels in the New Testament and notice the character qualities of Jesus. Strong yet gentle, tough yet tender, brilliant yet willing to speak so even a child could understand Him easily, Jesus was the perfect picture of power under control. He taught His disciples with His words, and He backed up His words with His life. Isn't it interesting that not one of the disciples of Jesus—not even Judas, the man who betrayed Him—ever said something like, "You know how Jesus talks? He doesn't really *live* that way." On the contrary, after spending three years with Jesus, night and day, in good times and bad, the disciples all said, "Did you hear what Jesus said? That is exactly the kind of person He is."

Jesus was the master teacher. He took every opportunity to teach His disciples how to live. In a similar way, to be a parent means that you are a teacher, instructor, leader, guide, confidant, communicator, and disciple-maker.

You may say, "What do you mean, *disciple-maker*?" The term *disciple* is the root word for *discipline.* To discipline means to instruct, teach, lead, or give someone the ability to develop. As a disciple-maker you are conforming your children to the things you hold to be right, pure, honorable, moral, and true.

KEEP UP WITH PROGRESS

As a parent who wants to be a wise, master teacher, you must also keep your eyes on your student's progress. Solomon, one of the wisest men who ever lived, said it best: "Know well the condition of your flocks, / And pay attention to your herds" (Proverbs 27:23). Keep an update on where your children are in their development, not just physically and emotionally, but in regard to staying within boundaries, taking responsibility, and maintaining accountability. It is a very foolish teacher who gives a test once a month, but doesn't keep up with the progress of the students between test times.

Every day is a test for our children; some are minor tests, some major, but each day of their lives, our children are being tested to find out what kind of students they are. We as parents are being tested as well, tested to find out what kind of parents we really are, and how well we are doing at establishing real boundaries for our children, applying discipline, and pointing out the way of life for them. In other words, we are being tested on our training discipline.

IT'S AN INDIVIDUAL THING

Our goal is to help bring the winner out in our child. If the very best your child can do is to be a trash collector, then help him become the best trash collector that has ever been. If your child has the ability to do more, fine—encourage him, keep your goal in mind. You want your children to become the best at whatever they choose, not what you would choose. I have met miserable doctors and lawyers and even preachers who wanted to do something else with their lives, but because their parents wanted them to pursue those careers, they allowed their parents' or someone else's dreams to dictate to them what their life's vocation would be. The vocations had their bodies and minds, but they did not have their hearts. Your children's vocational futures should never be linked to your pride or shame concerning their expressed areas of interest.

It may surprise some people to learn that my mother did not want me to start Big Oak Ranch. She was concerned that starting a ranch during this tumultuous time was not a good move. She advised against it. Perhaps your mom and dad have offered similar advice to you about some of your adventures and choices.

Even so, one truth that my parents had taught me kept tugging at my heart and mind. Mom and Dad had trained me to go for anything as long as I knew it was something I was supposed to do. I knew that starting Big Oak Ranch was something I was born to do. My dad eventually realized it too. It took a while longer to convince my mother, but today, she is my most loyal and vocal supporter. I am so glad my mom tempered her own concerns and did not try to squeeze me into her preconceived notions of what I should do with my life.

Not everybody is going to have a son who grows up to be a neurologist or a daughter who grows up to be a nuclear physicist, but we all can do our part to help our children grow up to be polite, courteous, courageous, and wise. We can teach them to be sound in their decision-making processes, to have character and commitment to God, and to have focus in their lives to help them stay on track. Those are the qualities of a winner.

These attributes do not suddenly develop when your child turns eighteen years old. Nor can you ignore matters of establishing boundaries and disciplining your child for sixteen years, and then suddenly decide that for the next two years before your child becomes an adult, you are going to pour these basics into him or her. Don't forget the fire-hydrant theory (Chapter 5). If you want to help bring the winner out in your child, you must start teaching discipline from your child's earliest days. Do not allow inexperience, uncertainty, or fear to paralyze your attempts to discipline your child. Do what you know is right.

START WHEN YOUR CHILD IS YOUNG

Just as we must begin establishing boundaries for our children when they are very young, we must also begin teaching them about discipline at a young age. Some parents object, "Oh, I don't want to discipline my child. She is just a baby. I don't want to upset her."

Of course, it is foolish to severely discipline a six-month-old. But it would be just as foolish to wait until your child is six years old to begin disciplining him or her. I have seen children with cuts and bruises because their parents waited too long to begin disciplining. When their parents finally began, they tried to make up for lost time, but they quickly moved from discipline and training to punishment and abuse. Such tragedies might have been avoided had the parents learned how to discipline with love, and had they started from the early days of parenting their child.

Many parents fear that if they start to discipline their children too early they will "break their spirits." Often these parents have a notion that human beings are basically good at heart, and if given enough time, love, a healthy environment, and a good education, they will turn out to be fine, disciplined people.

I disagree. Certainly, children need time, love, a healthy environment, and a good education. But in my years of working with children, I have never had to teach a child to be selfish. It comes all too naturally to children—and to all of us. Something within our nature causes us to lean not toward that which is good or right, as many naive parents assume, but toward that which is good for us. It is basic, raw selfishness, and it is usually seen in children as they begin, from the earliest moments of their lives, to express an "I want what I want when I want it" attitude. This attitude can be transformed, but the longer you wait to begin, the tougher the job. It is not impossible, but it is tougher.

At Big Oak Ranch, at any given time, we have a number of colts in our stables and in our pastures. Young children can walk up to our colts and pet them. From an early age, our colts are lovingly handled and touched by human beings. We usually put a halter on them when they are two or three days old. Although they are still frisky, our colts know from their youth that they must obey.

One time, a well-meaning friend gave Big Oak Ranch a stallion that had been in the pasture for five years, yet still wasn't "broken." What might have been a well-trained, useful animal, providing pleasure and enjoyment to many people, had become totally undisciplined and unusable. The horse could not function within his Big Oak Ranch society. Although the animal was a beautiful sight to behold, he was impossible to ride, and even dangerous to get near. He would kick or bite anyone who tried to control him. If a horse is allowed to live undisciplined for that long, and you think you are going to walk up and put a halter on it, you are going to have yourself the rodeo of your life!

Sadly, that is what many parents do with their children. They give them free rein throughout most of the child's early years. When at some point the parents attempt to put a "halter of discipline" on that child, they are often astonished that it is nearly impossible to break their child's selfish attitude.

Many of these parents realize they should have begun the disciplining process many years earlier. Some of the saddest words I hear parents of self-centered, rebellious, undisciplined children say are, "I don't know where my child learned to act like that," or "If only I had . . ."

Such comments, though sincere, misplace the responsibility. The child "learned to act like that" from you and me when we failed to correct the behavior at its earliest stages. You and I are responsible. We must start early to discipline our children for their own good. Imagine, for instance, that your toddler is reaching toward a hot stove. It would be foolish to say, "Well, I will simply let him learn for himself what a hot stove is all about." The child may be scarred for life. A wise parent would briefly explain to the child that the stove is hot and she is not allowed to touch it. A discussion of thermodynamics is unnecessary at this point. Remember to speak on your child's level of understanding. You can't be a giraffe and talk to sheep. Simply and firmly explain that the hot stove is dangerous and should be treated with respect. When your child reaches toward the stove, pull her hand away from it and say emphatically, "No! Do not touch!" If necessary, spank the child's hand as you pull it away. You may be reluctant to spank your child's hand, but the minor discomfort she feels from your discipline is far less than she would experience if she touched the hot stove. Repeat this process as often as needed until your child understands that touching the stove is off-limits.

How will you know the child has learned the lesson? The true test will come when you are out of sight. Only by backing away from the stove, yet staying close enough that you can intervene if necessary, will you know whether the child will continue obeying. Once trained, your child will never intentionally touch a hot stove. You did your job as a parent.

Imagine that same child when she is four years old. You now live near a busy street, and your child is playing with a ball in the front yard. The ball rolls out into the street, into oncoming traffic. You are on the front porch and you see the potential tragedy in the making and you know that you cannot get to your child in time. You yell at the top of your lungs, "Stop!"

What is the next line in this story?

If you have lovingly disciplined your child for the first four years of her life, when the child hears your voice calling, she will stop. If the child has not learned that there will be severe consequences for not stopping when Mom or Dad calls, you may witness the awful fruit of your not training your child in loving discipline.

Let's move ahead a few years. Imagine your child is now a teenager and she is in a car with a group of friends. The driver of the car is drunk and is trying to operate the vehicle. Will your child think, *I need to get out of this car. This is not a good situation*, or will she go along with the crowd?

The training you have given your children from the early stages will determine their decision in the moment of the testing.

WHEN YOUR CHILD
DOES NOT TELL THE TRUTH

Of the thirteen hundred children who have called Big Oak Ranch their home, 100 percent lied at one time or another, because to them, lying was a way of self-preservation. Lying was a way of getting things; lying was a way of weaseling out of things; lying was a way of getting out of trouble. We have had to teach our Ranch children that all lies are wrong, that lying always comes back to hurt them, that their lying will always catch up with them and, sooner or later, they will have to pay the consequences. Prisons and jail cells, as well as multitudes of unhappy homes, are filled with moms, dads, and children who have lived with lying.

At Big Oak Ranch, we place a high premium on truthfulness: For most children, lying is more than responding to impulsive desires, it is calculated deception. One of the key indicators that we are making a change in a child's life appears when he stops lying and starts consistently telling the truth.

Mom and Dad, you and I are probably no strangers to lying either. Who of us has not twisted the truth, concealed the truth, or left out important facts? We cannot go back and clean up all our errors from the past. But we can make up our minds to pursue the truth from now on. Regardless of past failures in this area, commit yourself today to a standard of truth in your life and in your home. Your mate and children are depending on you.

Reagan lied to Tee and me one time when she was very young. When we found out that she lied, we disciplined her appropriately. The discipline left an indelible impression upon her, so much so that it even impacted her younger brother, and he hadn't even been born yet! Years later, Reagan told Brodie all about the time she lied to us, and the way we disciplined her for it. Now she doesn't lie, and neither does Brodie! They have learned to tell the truth. In our house, we will tease, joke, and carry on, but when it is time to tell the truth, the truth is the truth. Sometimes we all mess up here, but we must work on this.

The Bible says, "There is no fear in love; but perfect love casts out fear, because fear involves punishment" (1 John 4:18). When you speak the truth and discipline in love rather than punish in anger, you no longer have to be afraid that your children will love you less because you have dared to discipline them.

CONSISTENCY, CONSISTENCY, CONSISTENCY

A second reason why we may be reluctant to discipline our children is our own inconsistency. It is tough to hold your child to a higher standard of conduct and values than you maintain in your own life. Can you honestly expect your children to heed your warnings to stay away from drugs when you are standing before them with a cigarette in your mouth or holding an alcoholic beverage in your hand? Your children will see straight through the inconsistencies between what you say and what you do. If you are going to teach positive values and character traits to your children, you must model them. Larry Christenson, a best-selling author of family-related books, wisely points out:

> Nothing is more important in establishing a parent's authority with the children than the example which the parent sets with his own life. . . . Parents must themselves be the embodiment of their teaching, if they want their authority to be established.[1]

In other words, you reproduce what you are.

WITHOUT CONSISTENCY, IT IS ANYONE'S GAME

All of the other positive parenting principles you may incorporate will be useless if you are inconsistent. You may be fair, firm, and loving, but if you are inconsistent in maintaining your child's boundaries or applying discipline when those boundaries are transgressed, your most valiant efforts will be in vain.

Mom and Dad, this is one of the most important keys to effective parenting: *You must be consistent!*

I described referees in Chapter 5 who vigilantly watch for repeat transgressions. There are others who fail to follow the same standards. Have you ever been to a baseball game in which the home plate umpire was inconsistent in his calls? Both teams soon become confused and frustrated.

Picture this: The batter steps up to the plate, and the pitcher throws a pitch almost into the dirt, but the umpire calls it a strike. The next time the hitter comes to bat, he is ready to swing at the low pitches, but now the umpire is calling strikes as high as the batter's shoulders. Both the pitcher and the batter are confused. They don't know where the strike zone is located. The resulting confusion creates an insecurity for everyone involved.

Similarly, when your children are uncertain as to when or how you are going to make the call concerning their boundaries and discipline, the result will be confusion and insecurity in their lives. Worse yet, they soon learn to play by their own rules.

Not long ago I attended a professional basketball game. Watching the referees make their calls was a classic lesson in inconsistency, especially when it came to the infraction known as "traveling" or "carrying the ball." The rules say that a basketball player can take only two steps before he must pass or shoot the ball. If he stops bouncing the ball, he cannot start again. He must pass or shoot it. Watching an NBA game, however, you would never guess that such rules exist. The players are aware of the rules, but because the referees are inconsistent in calling the infractions, you can never be quite sure whether a player's move was legal or not. Some referees allow the players to get away with taking more steps than two after their last bounce of the ball, especially if the player is "driving to the boards" and headed toward a slam dunk. Other referees call the infraction every time a player "travels." Certainly the players know better than to break the rule, but because of the inconsistencies in the officiating of the games, some of them will take advantage of every opportunity to score, regardless of the rules.

We are fooling ourselves if we think that something very similar does not happen when we are inconsistent in our parenting. Even though our children may know where the boundaries are, and what the consequences for breaking the rules are, if we are inconsistent in maintaining the boundaries and applying discipline when the boundaries are crossed, it will only be a matter of time before most children learn how to play the game by their own rules.

DIVINE DISCIPLINE

Discipline need not always be physically painful to be effective. Sometimes the most effective thing you can do is to lovingly look at your child and say, "Last night you were an hour late coming in. I was so frantic and worried. My heart was in my throat because I thought something had happened to you." The impact of this statement is predicated by the boundaries you have established, the discipline you have maintained, and the loving consistency with which you have administered the consequences of disobedience throughout your child's lifetime.

Your relationship with your child will determine how effective parental disappointment can be as a deterrent to incorrect conduct. Sometimes, if you show your children that you are extremely disappointed with them, it will break their hearts. Children love you and they know that you love them, so when they sense your disappointment, it crushes them. Instead of jerking them up and spanking them for inappropriate behavior, just letting them see your disappointment is often enough to let your children know they do not want to misbehave in that manner again.

Sometimes, however, we parents use disappointment as a

weapon and not a tool. We bludgeon our children with our disappointment and exaggerate how hurt we are, mournfully going on and on to the point that if we are not careful, our parental disappointment will lose its effectiveness. When it does, the danger is that you feel you must strike even harder blows with the weapon of disappointment. Be careful! Those blows are nonretractable.

Save disappointment for key times when it is most appropriate and it will have its greatest impact: in other words, those times when it is real. Even when it is real, be cautious in the way you use disappointment.

After all, you are not looking for a pity party (or at least you shouldn't be). What you are hoping to achieve is a change in your child's attitude that will result in a permanent change of performance and therefore will keep the child within the boundaries. If your child's attitudes are not changed, the inappropriate behavior will happen again, regardless of how disappointed your child might think you will become.

BE CAREFUL WITH YOUR WORDS

In all discipline, guard your words, your tone of voice, facial expressions, and your attitude. Any one of these can soothe or sting. They can build up, or they can tear down, bite, pummel, or rip. They can inflict irreparable wounds upon the self-esteem of our children if we are not careful. It is easy to fly off the handle when a child does something wrong. It is easy to say something thoughtless. For the sake of your child, hold your tongue until you are sure your words are under control.

Imagine that your child is a piece of rock and your tongue is the hammer and chisel in the sculptor's hands. Your tongue can be a tool used to make that child into a masterpiece, a person of exquisite beauty, or your tongue can be a weapon to mar, scar, and destroy that child. The choice is yours.

AVOID DISCIPLINE IN PUBLIC

We have all seen it. Right there in the middle of a busy shopping mall some mom or dad is whaling the tar out of a child. It makes us uncomfortable, and it should. We feel that we are eavesdropping on someone's personal business that would be better taken care of at home. "Now don't you let go of my hand in a store again," you hear the parent warn, "or you will get twice as much next time!"

"I certainly hope not," you almost want to say to the parent.

It is always better to discipline a child in private rather than in public. For one thing, discipline is a serious matter; at its best you do not merely want your child to stop misbehaving, you want your child to learn a lesson that will prevent such behavior in the future.

Furthermore, when you discipline in public you run the risk of the public misunderstanding or misrepresenting your actions. Although both you and your child may be aware of the reason you are disciplining the child, casual passersby may not. In the litigious society in which we live, you are leaving yourself wide open to accusations of child abuse or worse.

This is not to say that it is okay to beat your child as long as you do it in private. It is a sad reality, however, that many people nowadays might misinterpret your actions and your motives should you discipline your child in public. Besides, some things are simply handled better in a loving home atmosphere, and the discipline of your children is one of those things.

Beyond that, most parents tend to overreact when they discipline their children in public. Often this is the result of the embarrassment the child has caused the parent. In private, the parent has time to cool down, to think about the situation more objectively, and to ask him- or herself why the discipline

is necessary and what sort would best help t̶
the desired lesson.

Moreover, if you have to discipline you̶r ̶c̶
usually it is a sign that you have not done a very good jo̶b̶ ̶o̶
disciplining your child in private. The children of parents who
discipline in private usually are well trained before they get
into a situation that might tempt their parents to discipline in
public. Not that your children will never misbehave in public,
but if they do, they will be aware that there will be a price to
pay when they get home, or an immediate trip to some private
area where discipline will be applied.

In those situations where you feel you absolutely must discipline your child in public, whether by spanking or some sort
of restriction or taking away of a privilege, try to do so as
inconspicuously as possible. Do not make a scene. Do not try
to embarrass your child into behaving. It won't work. They
will win and you will lose! If not at the moment, then later on,
but trust me, you will lose! And whatever you do, do not discipline your child in front of their friends, not unless you wish
to alienate your child from you.

Understand that *shame* is not a proper tool to build the
character of a winner in your child. It will only lead to a
humiliating experience for your child. I have met with hundreds of children whose parents tried to shame them into sub-
mission. It never works.

DO IT FOR YOUR CHILDREN . . .
AND YOUR CHILDREN'S CHILDREN

We overcome our reluctance to discipline our children by
understanding first of all that they will not in fact reject us for
disciplining them; they will love us. Second, we earn the right
to feel comfortable and confident in disciplining our children
by being consistent in our lifestyle and our words. One of the

worst possible situations you and I could ever face is having our children realize we didn't discipline them or did not discipline them correctly, and they are now ill-equipped to be parents. For the sake of your children and their children, despite your fears and your own inconsistencies, it is imperative that you learn how to discipline your children in love. In the next chapter, I am going to give you some practical tips on how you can do that.

THE WINNER'S FOCUS

1. For what reasons have you been reluctant to discipline your child: fear that your child will not love you or inconsistencies in your own life? What steps are you going to take to overcome your reluctance to discipline?

2. Name at least two specific ways you can get off your child's back and onto their team.

3. Why is experience not always the best teacher?

4. What are some practical ways you can help your child learn the value of telling the truth?

5. Many people say "practice makes perfect." That old adage is not quite true. *Perfect* practice makes perfect performances. While we readily acknowledge that none of us are perfect, our goal is to do things right, and to practice doing them consistently, so our children will form habits that will help them live correctly. List four areas in which you can be more consistent in helping your child do what is right. Now list several steps you plan to take to accomplish these goals.

6. Every day we must walk what we talk so when a child steps out of bounds, we will not overreact or underreact. Imagine that your child has just crossed a boundary you have established. What steps are you going to take? How will you make the call? How will you discipline

the child for this imaginary infraction? It is important that we think through such situations before they happen. How will you explain to your children that they must practice running within the boundaries and play by the rules?

7. Think of some of the teachers and coaches who had the greatest positive impact upon your childhood. What disciplinary traits did they have in common? How many of those individuals were strong disciplinarians who cared enough for you to make you do things right, even when it was tiresome or troublesome? Whom do you respect more, the teachers and coaches who were hard on you or the ones who were soft on you?

8. Be extremely honest with yourself: Are you trying to impose your desires upon your children regarding their vocational futures, rather than allowing them to pursue those areas that most interest them, or in which they are gifted or called? What are some things you can do to make sure that your children are able to be what God has created them to be?

8

How to Apply
Discipline with Love

ONE OF THE MOST important keys to bringing out the
winner in your child is learning how to discipline in
love. Yet maintaining consistency, conveying absolute unconditional love and acceptance of your child, and administering
loving discipline all at the same time after a child's wrong-
doing are quite a tall order. It is not impossible, however.
Many parents confess to having a hard time doing this.

Often parents mistakenly choose to sustain their feelings
of love at the expense of discipline. On the other hand, some
misguided moms and dads actually feel that the only way they
can effectively discipline their children is by withdrawing all
signs of their love and emphasizing their anger and disappointment. Both of these extremes are destructive and ineffective methods of applying discipline that can have long-term
repercussions.

It helps to keep the goal of "discipline with a purpose" in mind. You are not merely disciplining your children for doing something wrong. You are hoping they will learn from the situation and choose correct behavior in the future as a result. Granted, it is not easy to administer discipline when your child is crying or misbehaving, or when you are feeling like a bowl of jelly yourself. But it must be done. This chapter will provide some practical ways of making your children mind without losing your peace of mind.

RESTRICTION

Restriction of your child's freedom to operate as he pleases is part of all discipline. In some cases, especially for minor incidents, restriction of some activity is all that is necessary to move your child from outside the lines back inside the boundaries. For instance, if your son fails to clean up his room, he may be restricted to the room until the room is cleaned. His buddies may all be sitting on the back porch waiting for him to go play ball. For your son, there will be no game until he conforms to the boundary you have previously set concerning his room.

Similar short-term restrictions can be used for most small boundary infractions. Notice, short-term restrictions should be designed for small infractions. For instance, you called your child in from the yard for lunch and you know she heard your voice, but she chose not to respond. When you get her attention, say, "Because you did not come immediately when I called you to come inside for lunch, you are not allowed out of the yard at all this afternoon. Tomorrow you may go with your friends to the playground, but the rest of today you will be restricted to the yard." Whenever restriction is used as a means of discipline, the child must be made to feel a sense of lost freedom.

Remember, restriction is best used for relatively short-term disciplinary measures. Restricting the amount of television viewing, or the number of social events your child can attend, may work when your child's school grades have dropped. Restriction should not be imposed for too long a period of time. If you say, "There will be no more television viewing for you, young man, until you get those grades up," you are setting a long-term restriction, rather than a short-term commitment to change. Most schools are on a six-week, twelve-week, or semester grading schedule. Are you prepared to restrict your child's television viewing for six weeks or longer? For some parents that may be feasible, but for most that would be an unrealistic restriction. After the first week or so, the restriction would be relaxed, if not forgotten altogether, and the discipline would be weak or ineffective.

Besides that, your child's grades may not be suffering because of too much television viewing. Slumping grades may be totally unrelated to television. Maybe—as hard as it is for most parents to believe—your child is simply not a whiz at math. His math grade may never improve. But you have restricted his television viewing until it does! Do not discipline your child when he is doing his best. Instead, brag on him for doing so well, when you *know* it is his best.

It would be wiser to say something such as, "Until I see some improvement in your study habits, you will be limited to one-half hour of television viewing per day." Your child's grades may or may not improve—they probably will—but at least you have not created a no-win situation with the restriction.

For younger children, you may restrict their activities merely by having them sit down next to you for a while. For older children, restrictions may be placed upon their taking part in after-school activities, dating, use of the family car, sports or community service club involvement, or any other meaningful area of your child's life. The lost freedom your children experience is a reminder to them when they choose to willingly and knowingly disobey you. Restriction is not punishment but discipline to change behavior.

TIME OUT

A popular method of discipline is the "time-out," a total restriction of the child's activities for a specific, brief period of time. It is just what it sounds like—an allotted amount of time during which you remove your child from her normal routine, requiring her to remain in her room or some other isolated place, away from the activities she enjoys doing. Sending children to their rooms for a time-out will be useless, however, if their rooms are where they normally go to watch television, play computer or video games, listen to their favorite music, or talk on the telephone. Even if your child has all the conveniences modern technology can provide, during a time-out, the use of all of these items must cease until you as the parent say the time of discipline has expired.

The fact that the child is not allowed out of the isolation room until you give the word is an important part of making a time-out an effective means of discipline. Do not simply say, "Go to your room," or even "Go to your room until you learn to behave." These instructions are much too general. Be specific. "You will stay in your room, with the door open, for fifteen minutes. Then we will talk about what you did and see if you are ready to come out of your room." If a child resists or cries, refuse to start the time-out clock until the child is settled and quiet. Keep your tone of voice and your overall demeanor kind and loving, not bitter, resentful, or angry. Your child needs to know that your love for her is not diminished in any way, but that you will discipline inappropriate behavior.

Once you have committed to a specific period of time for your child's time-out, do not alter or shorten it, no matter how much he or she protests, unless there are extenuating circumstances.

Be sure you are realistic in your time frame when you use a time-out as a form of discipline. The time-out should not be too short or too long.

Shorter time-outs can be used for younger children. Remember, you are not trying to punish your children, or conveniently keep them out of your hair while you are doing something else. You are calling your children's attention to the fact that because of their misbehavior, they have temporarily lost a certain amount of freedom. Personally, I have found the attention span of a child under ten is approximately one minute per year; an eight-year-old has an attention span of eight minutes. If you give a too-long time-out to a younger child, it will quickly lose its effectiveness because her attention span is so short.

Also, make sure you are specific when you describe the time period to your child. One time Brodie committed an offense, and I gave him a time-out as part of his discipline. It was about mid-afternoon. "You will stay in your room until suppertime," I ordered him.

"Yes, sir," Brodie answered dutifully. At 3:45 P.M. Brodie called my office and said, "Dad, come on home, it's time to eat supper!" I broke up laughing. But I learned to be more specific in setting the amount of time for future time-outs.

After the time-out has elapsed, you must talk with your child about what she did that led to the time-out. Do not merely allow your child out of isolation and back into the normal flow of the family life without helping her learn from this experience and to take responsibility for her actions. Remember, you are training your winner to win consistently.

Help her to understand that it was because of what she did that the discipline was administered. Let her know that more inappropriate behavior will result in more time-outs, possibly of longer duration. If you fail to discuss the meaning of the time-out, you have wasted both your time and your child's. You will have missed a window of opportunity to make a difference in your child's life. In discussing the reason for the time-out, you may also impose additional consequences that your child must face. "Because you broke your brother's toy truck, half of your allowance will be used to pay for the new toy." You must make your child accountable for her actions, and the sooner the better. This is tough love, but necessary.

Before allowing your child to resume her normal routine following a time-out, always assure her of your love and forgiveness. This is another good time for a hug. It brings closure to the situation and allows healing in what your child may regard as a fracture in her relationship with you. After all, you did banish her to her room for fifteen minutes! To an eight-year-old that seems catastrophic. Although it may seem like an insignificant amount of time to you, a child can stir up a lot of animosity in fifteen minutes. If there is no way to resolve those negative feelings, your child may emerge from her time-out with nothing more than anger or hurt feelings toward you, rather than a recognition of the reason for the discipline. Do not minimize conduct that got her into trouble. But be sure to offer plenty of affirmation, love, and forgiveness when the time-out is over. When your child has done the time for the crime, it's over.

Though time-outs work especially well with younger children, they can be used effectively even with teenagers if your child cooperates and willingly obeys your instructions concerning the isolation time. Once the child refuses to willingly go to the isolation room, or is too big for you to forcibly take to the isolation room, you must either find a better way of disciplining that child, or some stronger leverage that will cause him or her to willingly obey.

Use time-outs wisely to impress upon your children that their misbehavior has cost them a loss of time they could be enjoying some other way. Children do love their freedom!

GROUNDING

Grounding, restricting a child to home with few or no outside activities other than those absolutely necessary, is an especially effective method of discipline with teenagers. Again, however, the wise parent will not prolong the experience. Grounding a child for a day, a weekend, or even a week will leave a definite impression upon a child. A lengthy grounding will either lose its effectiveness or cause your child to feel resentment toward you. The lesson of the discipline will be lost during the process. Instead of training your winner, you will be losing the battle.

I know of parents who grounded their child for six months for making a mistake. After about two weeks, that child was frazzled and frustrated and had given up. His attitude was, "What's the use?" The grounding was too long. It was ineffective and confused the child.

The longest we have grounded any of our children at the Ranch has been a three-week period. We administered that grounding because school grades needed to come up. We told the child that he was grounded until the next set of grades came out, but we would have a review in three weeks to find out how he was progressing. If he was improving, we would lighten up and reward him for the progress he had made so far. On the other hand, if after that three-week period we discovered that the child was making little effort to improve, we would add more severe consequences such as more study time,

less play time, lost freedoms, and even removal from extracurricular activities.

As with the time-out and the restriction, you must discuss
the reason for the grounding and help your child learn from
the situation. Be brief, be fair, be consistent, and be done with
it once it is over. Discipline means you are training your child
to be better than before the incident occurred, so your child
will be prepared for the next test. As a parent, you will be better prepared too!

SPANKING

Because I have worked with children professionally for more
than twenty years, I have had numerous parents ask me, "Do
you think it is okay to spank children?"

My answer is, "Yes, when necessary and appropriate."

When you are trying to teach your child about potential
dangers, spanking may be necessary and appropriate. Imagine
there is a sharp knife on the counter and your little two-year-
old is repeatedly reaching for it. You say, "No, no!" If all your
child has ever heard is "No, no," the minute you turn your
back, that child is going to grab for that knife, and possibly
cut himself, something, or someone else. On the other hand,
if your child associates a sharp spank on the hand with that
"No, no," your chances of keeping your child from harmful
behavior are much greater.

Another time spanking your child may be necessary is
when your child deliberately disobeys or acts defiantly
toward you the parent. Mistakes, errors of judgment, and
other acts of childish irresponsibility can be disciplined in
other ways, but direct defiance toward a parent is definitely
grounds for a spanking.

Spankings should be infrequent. If you spank your child
for every little infraction, it will not be long before the child

becomes desensitized to it. Applied correctly, a well-earned spanking can produce wonders in a misbehaving child. Spankings should also be somewhat painful to the child. You do not want a spanking to be fun. Certainly, you do not want to overdo a spanking; you needn't whip a child violently or excessively. Yet to be effective, the spanking must cause discomfort; otherwise you may as well not do it. In most cases, a swat on the child's bottom which is padded with three inches of cotton diaper will not deter that child's misbehavior. A small switch on the back of the legs gains much attention. Once again, though, let me remind you to never discipline your child in anger.

Is there a danger of child abuse when parents spank their children? Yes, there is. We run the risk of inappropriate response when we cross the invisible lines between discipline, punishment, and abuse.

We have had many children at Big Oak Ranch who we knew came from abusive situations. In one case, after a thorough investigation, we discovered that a little boy's father would dislocate the boy's shoulder in his misguided attempts to discipline the child. The father knew the dislocation would leave no external marks on his boy.

How did he know that? His father had done the same thing to him. If you have ever seen a football game in which a young boy dislocates his shoulder, you will know how horribly painful this is. You can almost feel the injured player's anguish and pain all the way to the sidelines or in the stands. Can you imagine your own father doing that to you on purpose, and then having the cruelty to leave your shoulder dislocated for an extended period of time? That is exactly what happened to this young boy.

Ironically, many cases of abuse take place in homes where the child was not spanked until the parents became so angry, frustrated, and out of control that when they finally did attempt to discipline the child, it quickly led to abuse. To avoid overdoing a spanking, it is a good idea to use something other than your hand to apply it. A few swats with a ruler, a thin switch from a bush, or a small paddle works well. Besides lessening the physical power of the swats, the time it takes to go pick up a ruler or a switch or a paddle is often enough of a buffer to allow the parent to maintain or regain control of his or her emotions before spanking the child.

Spanking will *not* break your children's spirit, ruin their self-esteem, or cause them to turn into violent menaces to society if it is done in genuine love. In his classic book on child-raising, *Hide or Seek*, Dr. James Dobson, one of the leading psychologists of our time, concurs.

> Specialists [in child development] also say that a spanking teaches your child to hit others, making him a more violent person. Nonsense! If your child has ever bumped his arm against a hot stove, you can bet he'll never deliberately do that again. He does not become a more violent person because the stove burnt him. In fact, he learned a valuable lesson from the pain. Similarly, when he falls out of his high chair or smashes his finger in the door or is bitten by a grumpy dog, he learns about the physical dangers in his world. These bumps and bruises throughout childhood are nature's way of teaching him that the physical world around him must be respected. They do not damage his self-esteem. They do not make him vicious. They merely acquaint him with reality. In like manner, an appropriate spanking from a loving parent in a moment of defiance provides the same service. It tells him there are not only physical dangers to be avoided, but he must steer

clear of some social traps as well (selfishness, defiance, dishonesty, unprovoked aggression, etc.).[1]

Many times it is not so much the spanking itself that deeply affects children's behavior as it is their sensitivity to disappointing or upsetting their parents. "My mama spanked me," the child grieves. The child is brokenhearted, not because of the physical pain inflicted by the spanking, but because of the emotional hurt she feels. The child knows that she has hurt Mama's and Daddy's feelings, so she in turn feels badly. We have had children living at Big Oak Ranch who were not my natural children, but I knew the last thing those children ever wanted to do was to disappoint me. Of course, they did not want to receive a spanking, either!

Many of us grew up with parents who were from "the old school." We knew that if we got in trouble at school, for example, we would be in twice as much trouble at home. If we received a paddling at school (yes, Virginia, there was a time when teachers paddled students for misbehaving at school), we could expect a double portion of the paddle at home. Over the years, I have met thousands of parents who can attest to this being the pattern in their childhood experience. Of that number, less than a handful have told me their parents were abusive in administering the discipline. Today, those individuals are not warped; they are not oppressive, perverted parents. In many cases, they are some of the best parents I have been privileged to meet.

You may be thinking, "Well, I don't spank my child, and I never will." That is your choice, but in my experience, I have found that when children are raised without spanking, it is rare that they have the same values, respect, and solid foundation as those children who were raised in families where spanking was done in moderation and in loving discipline.

Simply put, if you associate misbehavior with pain, in most cases, the misbehavior will stop.

"No, no, Johnny. Don't do that" is not a painful enough experience to cause most children to correct their misbehavior. In fact, if a parent repeatedly tells a child, "I'm going to spank you if you do that," but then does not follow through on the warning, eventually that child loses faith in the parents and other adults around him. He begins to think the parents did not keep their word.

How much better everyone would have been if the parents had simply applied the "board of education" to the "seat of learning" in quick, decisive discipline.

Sometimes I have had to bring Ranch children into my office, and I have had to spank them. It was not fun. I did not really want to do it, but I knew it was my responsibility to administer discipline in their lives. Nevertheless, I wondered at times if we were having any positive impact upon those children at all. Nothing we did seemed to make a difference.

Years later, some of those same children, now grown adults, have come back to the ranch to see me. Inevitably one of them will say, "John, do you remember that time I went joyriding in the car and I was twelve and you spanked my behind?"

I say, "Yeah," wondering what is coming next.

"Well," they admit a bit sheepishly, "you know, I never forgot that. Thanks. It turned me around."

That is what we hope and pray for—that a real part of the discipline that we teach our children will remain with them, will have a positive impact upon them, and will help bring out the winner in them for the rest of their lives.

Taking Away a Privilege

With older children, time-outs, restrictions, and even grounding will sometimes not bring about the desired change in behavior. This is especially true as your children move toward adulthood and have their own jobs, spending money, and cars and are preparing to leave the "nest." When your job of packing your child's suitcase is almost done, sometimes the only effective discipline will be to take away a privilege. Certainly this method of discipline will also work with younger children, but as your child matures, taking away a privilege may be the only effective means of discipline.

Let me give you an example. I know a young man who was getting ready to take his car out and his parents said, "You are not going out."

He belligerently replied, "Oh, yes, I am!" and he got in his car and drove away. The dad was extremely angry, and he didn't know what to do. His son was almost an adult. He was much too big for spanking; time-outs and restrictions were out of the question, and the dad had little grounding power left. Suddenly he hit upon an idea.

When the boy came back, the dad looked at him and said, "I'm sorry that this happened. I'll deal with you in the morning."

The boy went to bed thinking that everything was okay, that he had won another battle with his dad.

When the boy came out the door to the driveway the next morning, he discovered to his surprise that his dad had moved the young man's car to the side of the driveway. The vehicle was jacked up and placed on blocks. His dad had taken all four wheels off the axles and hidden the wheels. The boy's car looked good, but it could not be driven. The dad had taken away the boy's privilege of driving that vehicle.

That young man learned a valuable lesson. The next time the boy says to his dad, "I'm going out," and his dad says, "No, you can't go out right now," that boy will stop and think, *Is the fun of the experience worth the price of the consequences?*

Sometimes the privilege you take away is something that everyone else in the family is able to enjoy. Dad says to Billy, "Son, did I not tell you to mow the lawn before I got home today?"

"Yes, Sir."

"Why didn't you do it?"

"I just didn't."

"And what did I tell you about not doing your chores?"

"You said if I didn't get my chores done, I would not be able to go roller-skating tonight."

"That's right. Now, your mother, brothers, and I are going roller-skating. We will drop you off at Grandmother's house, where you will stay until we are done. Because of your disobedience, you have lost the privilege of going skating with us tonight."

Once we were having problems at Big Oak Ranch with a seventeen-year-old boy named Ben. The boy had come to us from an extremely fragmented family, a home in which there was little respect for the parents. Consequently, Ben had a bad habit of "smarting off" to his houseparents.

Because of his age, spanking was out of the question as a viable means of discipline, and most other forms of discipline failed in achieving any measurable change in his attitude or his sassy mouth. He was beginning to have a profoundly negative impact upon the other children living in that home, so I knew we could not tolerate Ben's insolence much longer. The next time I heard about him smarting off to his houseparents, I called Ben in and told him as firmly as I could, "If you smart off around here, there will be serious consequences." Ben knew that my words were not a threat; they were a promise.

Unfortunately, that did not keep him from talking back to his houseparents that night. When I heard about it, I knew I had to do something. But what could I do to discipline this boy in such a way that he would learn a positive lesson?

We were scheduled to leave for our annual Ranch trip to Florida the following morning. The trip is a highly anticipated time of fun and sun for our children, and it is one of the highlights of our year. I knew that Ben, like all of our children, was looking forward to going. Although I rarely discipline our children in public, I decided Ben was going to be an exception to the rule.

The time finally arrived for our departure and all the children were in the big bus, seated and ready to begin our great adventure. I boarded the bus and stood at the front to make an important announcement.

"Ben!" I called to the seventeen-year-old seated with his friends in the back of the bus.

"Yes, sir?"

"Did you smart off to your housemother last night?"

Almost instinctively Ben sensed trouble. "Oh, I was just kidding."

"What did I tell you about smarting off?" I pressed.

"Well, you said something, er, ah, I don't know, something about getting me if I smarted off again. . ."

"All right, Ben. Get off the bus."

"What?"

"You heard me; get your suitcase and get off the bus. I told you that if you smarted off one more time, there would be consequences. Now, we are going to Florida for the next few days, and you will stay here with the staff members who are remaining at the Ranch. You will have your regular chores to do every day while the rest of us are enjoying our time on the beach."

"But that's not fair . . ." Ben began to protest.

"It is perfectly fair. Now get off the bus," I said without any hint of a smile.

With fifty-nine other boys watching, Ben gathered his things and got off the bus. The bus pulled out for Florida, and we left Ben standing with our staff members in the driveway.

That was the last time we ever had a problem with Ben smarting off. Beyond that, the lesson Ben learned profoundly affected many of the other boys on the bus that day. Taking a privilege away from Ben was the only way we could get his attention, but once we had it, Ben began to turn around in a positive direction.

WHEN YOUR BEST ISN'T GOOD ENOUGH

The best advice I can give you when it comes to disciplining your children is to expect mistakes. Don't expect perfection from yourself or from your child. When you mess up, admit it and correct it. Our job as parents is to teach our children how to be honest, to admit their shortcomings, mistakes, and failures, and to learn from them. We must understand and accept this as part of training. The purpose of training for both your child and you is to lower the number of mistakes and the severity of these mistakes. It is also the time to practice doing things right.

Just as there are no perfect parents, there are no perfect children. I would love to say Tee's and my children, Reagan and Brodie, are perfect, but they are not; I would love to tell you that the thirteen hundred children who have lived at Big Oak Ranch are perfect, but they are not. I would love to tell you that our methods of discipline always work. Sometimes, they don't.

Over the years, most of the children who have lived at Big Oak Ranch have gone on to lead productive lives. Our success stories are numerous and inspiring. Occasionally, however, despite our best efforts, a child remains incorrigible. We do our very best to love, teach, and encourage the child, to discipline as necessary, to help him or her in every way, yet for some reason, he or she simply does not respond. Our best wasn't good enough.

In those cases, I must take extreme measures. It hurts me deeply to have to tell a young boy or girl, "You are going to have to leave." I know for many of them, there are few places in this world where they can go and find what we are giving them at the Ranch—a chance. Nevertheless, at times when all our efforts fail to help a child, for the sake of the other children who are living at the Ranch, we will issue an ultimatum to a child: "One more serious problem, and you are out of here."

Issuing the ultimatum is tough enough. Following through on it is even harder. When necessary, we do. Randy was such a case.

Randy was always in trouble. I had warned Randy again and again that he had to straighten up and obey his houseparents and the rules of the Ranch. All of our attempts to discipline him proved useless. One day, after Randy had done something else to totally upset his houseparents, I put my arm around Randy's shoulder and said, "Come on, Randy. Let's take a little walk." The two of us walked out the long lane leading to the Ranch, until we got to the entry. We stopped there, turned around, and looked back at the bustling Ranch behind us. Above the entry to the Ranch was a sign that read, "A Christian Home for Children Needing a Chance."

I pointed to that sign and in a last-ditch effort, I said, "Randy, I am the best friend you have ever had, but now you are down to one last chance. If you disobey your houseparents or disrupt your family in a serious way again, I am going to send you away. You have left me no other choice. Do you understand, Randy?"

"Yes, sir," Randy replied contritely. As we walked back to the Ranch, where the other children were busy playing ball, racing their bicycles, and participating in a host of other activities, I thought, *Maybe this time Randy is going to go straight.*

I was wrong. It was only a matter of days before Randy was in my office again because of a serious breach of his boundaries. I went through the same process I have described, asking the questions: "Did you know what you were doing? Did you understand that there would be unpleasant consequences for your actions? Did you realize that this was your last chance?"

We had been down this road before, and Randy and I both knew it. I had warned the boy again and again, until I had finally given him an ultimatum. Now I had to stick to my word. It was time to act. I told Randy that he would have to leave Big Oak Ranch. We would be sending him away to a more structured environment. It broke my heart, but I said nothing as I watched him go.

About a year later, I was driving along a country road, and I saw a familiar face. Sure enough, it was Randy. He was picking up soda cans, I assume to take to a recycler so he could earn some money. Randy recognized my truck and waved as I approached. I barely slowed down long enough to wave back. It made me sad to pass by that boy, but Randy had made his choice. I had a Ranch full of boys and one full of girls who desperately wanted and needed what Randy had squandered away. . . . But those thoughts did not make it easier to pass him by.

People often ask me what the toughest decisions are that I have had to make since opening Big Oak Ranch. The second toughest decision I have had to make is when we had one bed available and thirty children on a waiting list. The absolute toughest decision I have had to make was to look in the eyes of one of our Ranch children and realize that he had not responded in any way to our training. I had to remove that child from one of our homes and send him to another location.

On the other hand, at Big Oak Ranch we never close the door completely if a child shows interest and potential for returning. Once we had to remove an eighteen-year-old boy named Jim because he would not abide by our house rules and he refused to change after repeated warnings. We tried everything we could to reach Jim, but his rebellious attitude and flagrant rejection of our rules forced us to ask him to leave. Anxious to get out on his own anyhow, Jim agreed enthusiastically.

Six months later he came to see me. He asked straightforwardly, "Can I come back?"

"Jim, there are two things we need to discuss before I answer your question," I replied. "First, our rules have not changed, and they are not going to because of you. If we allow you to come back, you will be required to abide by the rules of the house. Do you understand that?"

"Yes, sir; I do."

"Second, I want to know, has your heart changed? Has your attitude improved? Are you willing to abide by our rules?"

With chilling sadness in his voice, Jim replied, "No. My heart hasn't really changed."

I looked back at him with regret but also with resolve. I knew that I could not compromise our rules. The words did not want to come out, but I finally answered, "I appreciate your honesty, Jim. I'm sorry. You cannot come back. When your heart changes and you can live by our rules, you are welcome, but not until then. The door is open, but the next move is up to you."

As an alternate example, we had one boy who was causing problems and who eventually left us to live with relatives. After three months he called me and asked me to meet with him. When I saw him, he asked if he could come back and live at the Ranch.

My first question was, "Do you know that your heart has got to change and that our rules have not changed?"

He replied that all he thought would happen with his relatives had not worked out and that he was sorry for the way he had acted. Then he simply said, "Can I have another chance?"

I looked at him and assured him he had that chance as long as his heart was changed.

The boy lived here another five years and is now out on his own and doing well. Again, always leave an open door.

If an older child refuses to abide by your rules, you may need to inform the child that she will not be welcome to remain in your home unless she obeys you. If you are a single parent, or if your physical stature or emotional makeup is such that you cannot enforce such an ultimatum, you might need to enlist help from a friend, a family counselor, your pastor, or possibly even the police.

It always hurts when you know your best efforts have failed. Remember, however, the game is not over yet. It may well be that your uncompromising commitment will be what God uses to get a child's attention and turn her around in the right direction. When you have done your best and your best does not seem good enough, all you can do is pray, commit that child into the Lord's hands, and trust God to bring her to her senses.

DONE IS DONE

Regardless of the form of discipline you choose to use with your child, one important principle cannot be overemphasized: When you have disciplined your child, and you have discussed the purpose for the discipline, your future expectations, and the desired conduct, everything regarding that infraction is done; it is over. Do not bring the incident up again. Do not throw your children's failures back in their faces by saying, "Well, do you remember when . . . ?"

Only bring up past incidents of discipline if there is a positive circumstance or a positive lesson associated with it that you want your child to remember. When the matter of the crossed boundary has been dealt with, it is over and done, regardless of how severely your child has hurt your heart, crushed your spirit, or damaged a possession. More important, once it is over it is time for you to forgive your child and express that forgiveness. Forgiveness is not simply a feeling; it is a choice you must make. You may never forget the pain or the hurt of the experience, but don't keep using it as a weapon against your child. Choose to forgive, choose to forget, and move on.

A friend of mine, Clebe McClary, is an internationally known speaker and motivator, and decorated Vietnam War veteran. His body was mutilated by a mortar shot in a firefight in Vietnam; Clebe lost his arm and part of his face. It took thirty-three operations and more than two and a half years to put what was left of him back together. Clebe has a favorite saying posted on the front license plate of his car—FIDO. Forget It, and Drive On! If anyone would have a reason to remember hurts from the past and to be resentful, it would be Clebe. Instead he chooses to forget the past and drive on.

The most forgiving people in the world are your children. In most cases, they have not yet learned the adult habits of covering their feelings or holding on to bitterness and resentment. They usually do not harbor feelings of revenge. They will forgive you for almost anything, except not trying to be a good parent, and not being willing to discipline them.

That is why it is important that we understand that no is not a four-letter word. In the next chapter, we will discover that saying no to our children can actually be a positive experience—for them and for us!

THE WINNER'S FOCUS

1. In what ways have you disciplined your child because you have been embarrassed rather than because of the offense?
2. Which of the various methods of discipline do you think would be most effective with your child? Why?
3. What are your feelings about spanking? What are values of spanking? What are its dangers?
4. Why is it so important that you express forgiveness for your child's infractions after the discipline has been applied?
5. How has reading this chapter affected your thoughts concerning disciplining your child?
6. Remember, exhaust all possibilities and be sure you have done your best before you issue the ultimatum that your child cannot live in your home. Once that line is crossed, only your child's change of heart will allow you to change your decision. Are you sure you have done your best? If not, what steps are you going to take to remedy the situation?

9

It's Okay to Say No

*J*OEY! DON'T YOU DARE touch that candy!" Joey's mother, Audrey, called from the family room. "It will ruin your supper."

Eight-year-old Joey jerked his hand away from the box of chocolates sitting on the kitchen counter. But he was not about to give up that easily. "Oh, please, Mom, can't I have just one?"

"No, I told you. I have a good supper almost ready. As soon as Daddy gets home we are going to eat, so I do not want you to spoil your appetite by eating candy right now. Besides, you know that candy is not good for you. It will rot your teeth out."

Joey ran his tongue over his front teeth. *Mmm, teeth . . . candy; candy or teeth*, he thought. The candy won easily.

"But one piece won't hurt," Joey whined.

"I told you, no. How many times do I have to tell you?"

"I'll eat my green beans, Mom, I promise. Can't I just have one little piece of candy?"

"Oh, all right," Audrey relented. "I suppose one little piece won't hurt anything. But only one. And make it a small one," Audrey called, as she turned her attention back to the book she was reading in the family room.

Joey reached for the chocolates. He picked out the largest piece in the box. And then because his fingers had "accidentally" touched another large piece, he popped that piece into his mouth too.

If Audrey doesn't soon learn that it is okay to say no, and to stick to it, she is going to have a lot more serious problems with Joey than simply tooth decay. But Audrey is not alone. Many modern-day parents need to know that it is okay to say no to their children. No is not a four-letter word!

Imagine what is going to happen to Joey when he is fourteen years old and the junior high physical education teacher says, "No, you may not climb that rope today." The teacher leaves the gymnasium to answer a telephone call and what does Joey do? He is up that rope in a flash. What Joey does not know, however, is that the rope is frayed at the top, and it is not safe. But by the time Joey gets near enough to the top to see the fray, it is too late. The rope snaps and Joey plummets to the floor, breaking his back. He is permanently paralyzed with no hope of ever walking again. Joey's injury quite possibly could have been avoided had Audrey and Joey's dad taught their son to respect the word no.

We live in the country and it is common knowledge that you cannot have two bulls in the same barn. What I mean is, either the parent is in charge, or the child is in charge. If you are going to be in charge, you must recognize that it is okay to say no, to establish boundaries, and to discipline your child when he breaks the rules. You must help your child to understand that when you say no, you mean it, and you say it not because you are unfair or do not understand your child's circumstances, but because you as the parent have weighed the available information and made the best decision possible.

INSIDE INFORMATION

One reason why we say no to our children as they are growing up is because we have more practical knowledge, wisdom, and experience than they do. Often you have knowledge about a particular situation of which your child is not aware. That information weighs heavily on your decisions concerning what you allow or disallow your child to do.

Consider this: I am the leader at Big Oak Ranch, but I am not everybody's best friend. Why? Because every day I have to make tough decisions that somebody is not going to agree with or be happy about. But as I make those decisions, I usually have much more information at my disposal than anyone else at the Ranch. I have people around me who have the ability and resources to help me make wise decisions. And I am responsible to make the right decision.

You are the leader of your home, and you, too, have to make decisions that are not popular. But you know more information than your children and must be strong when you know it is necessary. Say you're at the table with your six-year-old son. He has vegetables on his plate, not the hot dogs or pizza he would prefer regardless of nutritional value. He may argue and fuss, but you know it's in his best interest to eat vegetables, fruits, and other good foods versus pizza at every meal. You have made the right decision.

Then again, sometimes I make what I think is a good, wise decision and the next day receive a new set of facts that change my mind on the matter completely. For example, Billy, a boy who lived at the Ranch, was driving home when he lost control of his car and wrecked. Billy escaped unharmed but the mishap did some serious damage to Billy's car. At first glance, it appeared that the reason Billy wrecked was because he was driving too fast for the road conditions. When I confronted him about it, Billy said, "I don't understand that. I don't think I was driving too fast."

Nevertheless, I told Billy, "Because you were irresponsible, I am taking your keys for one month."

Billy protested, but I had made my decision.

The next morning, Jimmy, the equipment manager at Big Oak Ranch, came in to tell me that after further investigation, he had discovered that Billy had blown his right front tire. That was the reason he had lost control of his car.

I had based my decision to discipline Billy on facts I had been given the day before. Now I had a completely new set of facts that changed my position and the position I needed to take toward the child. There is a time for irrevocable steadfastness, and there is a time for merciful flexibility. This was the latter.

I called Billy in to my office and told him, "Billy, I have changed my mind. I have just found out that you had a tire blow out on your car. That was the reason you lost control. That sort of accident could happen to anyone. Because of this new information, here are your keys back. Now, be careful, and make sure you have good tires on that car."

That was not being wishy-washy. That was discerning the facts and making the correct decision. In this case, the correct decision required me to reverse my previous decision because I had a new set of facts.

When Robert Lutz, the president of the Chrysler Corporation, came to visit Big Oak Ranch, he and I had a long talk about the responsibilities we carry for making the right call. I said, "Robert, I'm sure glad I don't have to do what you do. You have so many people depending on you to make the right choices."

"Oh, yes, but you do too," said Robert. "What I decide every day affects half a million people, so I weigh each decision carefully. Many times, some people who are working in our offices or in our factories or in our showrooms may not like the decision I have made, but I have all the facts in front of me. They do not. What I do may affect more people, but in a way, you are doing the same thing, only on a smaller scale."

Sometimes your best efforts and decisions will not be understood by your children. Many times it is counterproductive for you to try to explain everything about why you say no to your children, but when you base your call on facts that your children do not have, they need to trust you.

Here is another example. Pete refuses to allow his ten-year-old son, Matt, to go to a party at Scott's house on Friday night. Why? Because Pete knows something that Matt does not. Pete knows that Scott's dad is a drug dealer, and Pete does not want his son to be in that environment. Pete prefers not to cast aspersions on Scott's dad. Rather than lying about the situation or concocting a superficial reason about why Matt is not allowed to attend the party, Pete chooses to remain silent. He is adamant, however, that Matt stay away from Scott's house. That is all Matt needs to know.

Suppose that Pete was reluctant to say no to Matt when he asked to attend the party at Scott's house. Perhaps Pete was afraid that his son would not love him if he refused to allow him to go, or maybe Pete was afraid to refuse Matt's request because Pete thought Matt might pitch a temper tantrum if he could not attend the party. For whatever reason, suppose Pete did not say no, and Matt attended the party.

At Scott's party, a group of fourteen-year-olds illegally obtained half a case of vodka and, as a joke, they were having a contest to see who could drink the most the fastest. They pressured Matt into drinking some. One of the older boys had a small amount of cocaine, and as a sort of initiation to the group, coerced Matt into taking some.

A few hours later, Pete was called to identify the body of his son at the morgue. The father had lost his son because he was afraid to say no.

Pete and Matt's story is hypothetical. Across America every day, similar tragedies take place. Only *those* tragedies are real-life incidents.

During your child's early years especially, it is better to use short, direct yes or no responses to your child's requests. When you say no, do so with a gentle, loving expression and tone of voice, but be firm. You will save yourself and your child many hassles later in life if your child realizes at an early age that Mom and Dad have a right to make absolute, uncontested choices for them.

As the child matures, it is sometimes appropriate to explain the reason why you are saying no. If Matt were age sixteen, it might be appropriate for Pete to explain his decision to his son.

If you can do so without hurting someone else or compromising your position as the parent, your explanation will help your child to realize that you are not merely making arbitrary decisions. But do not defend your decisions to your child. Do not allow your child to be disrespectful or to attack you when you make a decision. A good motto is, "Explain, yes; defend, no."

What is the difference? Simply put, defending your reasons for saying no usually ends up being argumentative. We tend to defend our decisions when our own confidence is questioned or shaken. "No, you cannot wear that dress because I will be the laughingstock of the town." Explaining, on the other hand, is informative and provides insight into the need for the refusal. "No, you cannot wear that dress, because you have high moral standards, and that dress makes you look as though you are willing to compromise those standards."

When you feel you must defend your decision, you are not secure in your decision. You are not confident in your role as the parent, in your decision-making process, or in the decision itself.

The true definition of a leader is that he is confident in two things: He knows where he is going, and he is able to persuade others to go with him.

I know parents who know exactly where they want to go, but they cannot persuade anyone in their family to go with them. There are also parents who can get the family to go with them, but they don't have a clue where they are going. Your children will know the difference. A confident parent explains but does not defend his or her decisions.

Do Not Let Temper Tantrums Intimidate You

Many parents are good at saying the initial "No," but when their child responds by pitching a temper tantrum, the parents' resolve melts away. Some parents are easy prey to a tantrum-pitching child because the parents are embarrassed that another adult will hear the child wailing and think less of the parents. Other parents may fear that they might actually be traumatizing their child by igniting the tantrum. Regardless of the reasons, many parents back down in the face of a loudmouth, bratty child. I have one question, Mom and Dad: Who is in charge of your home?

A mother came to me and said, "What am I going to do? My child is destroying our home. Our family cannot go out to eat, we can't go to a show, my husband has left, my oldest child is ready to leave, and my other children do not want to be at home. This child's outbursts are ruining our family."

I asked the woman, "How old is your child?"

She answered, "He is four years old."

At Big Oak Ranch, we keep some of our bulls in stalls. Imagine, though, if those strong-willed animals were kept in a stall with three concrete walls and the fourth wall was made of plywood and cardboard. If the bull pitches a tantrum and rams one of the concrete walls, he will quit doing it before long. Why? Because he is getting a headache! Unless the bull is mentally, emotionally, or chemically imbalanced, that bull will stop his tantrum once he hits the wall. On the other hand, if that bull hits the plywood and cardboard wall, we have a lot of bull running around loose.

Children are the same way. If a tantrum works and they get what they want, they'll do it again and again. But the wise parent realizes this has to stop. Many children are bullheaded when it comes to trying to get their way. You must stop those tantrums in their tracks.

It is not wrong for you as the parent to allow your child to express the frustration or anger he may be feeling, but do not allow defiant, disrespectful behavior based upon rebellion. If your child is the tantrum-throwing sort, wait until the initial wave of the outburst subsides, then in a loving but firm manner, look your child right in the eyes and say something such as, "Darling, I know you are very upset, and I think we should talk about what you are feeling. Most children get angry with their parents once in a while, especially when they feel Mom or Dad hasn't treated them fairly. But because I love you so much, I cannot allow you to scream, yell, bite, kick, call names, or throw any other sort of temper tantrum. If you continue to throw a fit, I will have to discipline you."

When you have the courage to fulfill your responsibility and tell your children no, you are not warping their personalities; you are preparing them for life in the real world. Imagine the four-year-old girl who is told no, but when she pitches a temper tantrum her mom or dad backs down. When the child is fifteen years old she is told no and she once again responds by pitching a temper tantrum. Once again, Mom or Dad caves in to the child's outbursts. Ten years later, our little girl is now a twenty-five-year-old woman, and she is working in the business world. When she is told no, she responds much as she did as a child—by pitching a temper tantrum. In the workplace, however, a temper tantrum will probably cost her the job. Just as easily, her temper tantrums might destroy her marriage relationship or her relationship with her children.

DON'T SAY NO AUTOMATICALLY

Although as parents most of us want to say yes to our children as much as possible, we tend to do just the opposite. That should not surprise us. After all, we live in a world that sometimes seems terribly negative. Beyond that, it is easy to get into a habit of saying no to our children almost as a reflex action. We say no dozens of times each day, without hardly thinking about it.

"No, you may not stay after school to play basketball."

"No, you may not have another cookie."

"No, you cannot go outside to play."

"No, you may not go to the movies." "No, you do not need a new bicycle."

"No, you may not stay overnight at your friend's house."

"No. No. No!"

"Dad, may I . . . ?"

"No, don't even think about it!"

Sometimes we are so preconditioned to refusing our children's requests that we may not even have a good reason for saying no; we simply say it on general principles. It just seems like the right answer. After a while, saying and hearing no tends to be depressing for both the parent and the child.

The title of this chapter notwithstanding, most parents need to seek more ways to say yes to their children more frequently. It will make saying no when it counts much easier. Often, even when you must say no, some affirmative response is possible.

"Yes, you may have a cookie . . . after you have eaten your lunch."

"Certainly you can go outside to play, but not until your homework is done."

"No, you can't stay overnight at your friend's house tonight. This is a school night. Maybe you can stay over on Friday night if it is okay with your friend's parents."

Say yes to your child as much as possible, and then you will be less reluctant to say no when you must. When it is important for you to refuse a request your child has made, do not back down; do not be afraid to be the boss. Although it flies in the face of much of the advice many modern "parenting experts" espouse, your children need to know that there is someone stronger, wiser, and more experienced in the family than themselves, someone with the backbone necessary to say, "No, you may not have that," or "No, you may not go there," or "No, you may not do that." As strange as it may seem, children are sometimes their own worst enemies and need to be protected from themselves. Part of your job as the parent is to love your children enough to exercise your better judgment in training and protecting them. Your children may protest loudly—weeping, wailing, and gnashing teeth—but deep down, especially in future years, they will appreciate that you love them enough to say no when necessary.

Kurt is sixteen years old, has all the latest video games,

CDs, and tapes, wears expensive designer clothes, and drives a late model Corvette to school every day. His parents buy him almost anything he wants. They allow him to come and go freely, and never require him to do chores around the house or be home at a certain time.

Amazed at Kurt's lifestyle, one of his friends said, "Man, Kurt. Your parents are really great!"

Kurt thought for a moment and then replied, "Really? My parents have never told me no. They really don't care what I do, just so I'm out of the house."

Interesting, isn't it? A boy whose parents give him every material trinket they can purchase desperately needs his mom and dad to say no once in a while. Your children do too.

HOW TO SAY NO IN LOVE

The courage to say no to your children is nothing more than assuming your God-ordained position as the parent. It is not easy to make right decisions, regardless of the costs, but the rewards are eternal. While you want to say yes as often as possible, you cannot say yes all the time. It is not healthy. It is inevitable that you will encounter situations that absolutely demand you to say no to your children. Nevertheless, it is possible and desirable to do so positively. Your children come away from the refusal feeling good about themselves and confident in your love for them. Here are a few tips that will help:

Listen Before You Leap

Be sure to pay close attention when your child is describing the event or situation in which he would like to participate. Recognizing that you may be predisposed to say no, force yourself to give your child the benefit of the doubt. Carefully consider your answer before jumping to conclusions or making snap judgments concerning the request.

Many requests do not require a great deal of time for you to make up your mind whether you want your child to be involved. Known trouble spots in town—and every town has them—are out of the question. Illegal activities such as using the car to drive to school without a license, plagiarizing an article for a report, dangerous activities such as attending parties at which alcohol is available to underage drinkers, or activities that promote drug usage or sexual immorality should be rejected without dispute. Nevertheless, hear out your child's request.

For example, if your thirteen-year-old child wants to attend a rock concert at which you know there will be ready access to drugs, or the performance will involve sexually explicit actions, language, or lyrics, you would be foolish to allow your child to attend. Instead of rejecting his request without considering it, however, first inform him of your concerns (don't be surprised if he does not see the danger or agree about the potentially harmful nature of the performance), and try to use the situation to clarify your values regarding some unacceptable contemporary music. If at all possible, offer an alternative event to attend. "I don't think that show is one you should go to, but there is another concert coming up that you can attend." When you offer an alternative, be sure it is something exciting to your child, not simply to you.

Turn the Volume Down

When you must say no to your child, you need to speak in a calm, confident tone of voice. Of course you want to convey authority, assurance, and firmness, but that doesn't mean you need to yell loudly or excitedly as you refuse your child's request. By keeping your voice low and without strong emotion, you are more likely to avoid having your refusal escalate into an ugly confrontation with your child.

Be careful of your body language too. Grimaces, grunts, groans, sighs, and smirks all convey as much or more than your words. Also, if at all possible, look your child in the eyes as you say no. Do not allow yourself to make sweeping, casual decisions about your child's requests while you are reading, watching television, or talking on the telephone. When your child has a request, give him your full attention. That way, even if you must say no—even when you know what the answer will be before your child finishes—your child's self-worth will remain high. He will feel that you gave the matter careful consideration. This attention is imperative to expressing your love.

Say No to Something Rather Than Someone

When you must say no, be careful that you do not cast aspersions on your child or your child's friends. Be especially cautious concerning your child's self-image. Avoid statements such as, "You are way too small to do that," "You'd poke your eye out if I let you do that," "You could never do that right," or similar demeaning comments.

Similarly, avoid making negative statements about your child's friends as you are saying no. "That Johnny Jones is no good. I do not want you going to his house after school." A possibly better way to say the same thing is, "I can't let you go to Johnny's house till I know more information."

Most important of all, when you say no to your children, you must emphasize the distinction between refusing your children's request and rejecting the child. They must understand that although you are saying no to their request, you are not rejecting them as a person. Your love for your children is still very much intact and is being expressed, even though you cannot go along with your children's desired conduct or request.

For example, your child requests to see a particular movie that is not within your family's ratings boundary. Your family's standard is PG, but the movie is NC-17. A negative response would be "No, you can't go! And I can't believe you would even ask to go. What kind of child am I raising?"

Obviously a poor choice of words. A better response might be "Son, what I've heard about that movie and its content is unacceptable, and no, you can't go."

Even if you must refuse your child's request, you want your child to feel comfortable in approaching you the next time she has a question. If you slam the door in your child's face with no explanation or discussion—"I said no, and that's final. Don't ask me again!"—do not be surprised if your child simply does not bother to ask you the next time she wants to do the same thing. Remember, it is okay to say no, but do so in a manner that does not create barriers to future communication between you and your child.

Communication is the key to all good relationships, and this is especially true in your relationship with your child. In his excellent book, *Raising Positive Kids in a Negative World*, popular motivational speaker Zig Ziglar suggests several ways parents communicate with their children:

> Our body language indirectly says a lot, and we communicate directly with the spoken word and the amount of time we spend with them. The most positive or negative communications, as far as results are concerned, take place when parents talk about their children. How the parent really feels about the child is often revealed in the discussions either in the child's presence or ostensibly when the child is not listening. The kids believe this overheard conversation and respond accordingly.

I've heard parents call their kids monsters or dummies. I've heard parents say such cruel and thoughtless things as, "When he failed the third-grade reading test, I knew we were going to have trouble with him and that he would never be a good student. He does such dumb things in school, but that's to be expected; he does dumb things around the house." . . . You can be certain that what your child hears you say about him will be taken at face value, while the words you say to him are often taken with a grain of salt.[1]

POTENTIAL "NO" AREAS

Television

The majority of modern American children spend more time watching television than any other single activity, including school or interacting with family members. Consequently, no single medium holds more potential for negatively influencing your child than the television programs you allow into your home. We have grown numb to statistics that once shocked us concerning the enormous number of murders, attempted rapes, robberies, and immoral sexual situations the average American child sees by the time he is twelve. Nevertheless, more than ever before, parents need to practice saying to their children, "No, you may not watch that sort of program."

Besides being a robber of time and creativity, and an enemy to real communication among family members, television pummels your children with messages that are becoming increasingly hostile to the family unit. While many parents are vigilant about prime-time viewing, the input that is most dangerous to your parental authority may well be coming from the cartoons and children's programs aired by networks thought to be "safe" by many parents. The negative influence of television programming is particularly offensive to many of the values most parents hold dearly. An article in *The Mediator*, the newsletter of Mastermedia International, Inc., a Hollywood "watchdog" organization, points out:

> It's not Big Bird and the Cookie Monster. It's a kids' show called *You Can't Do That on Television*; it's talk of "nice juicy booger" with kids in mock vomiting. Forget the sweetness of *Mr. Rogers' Neighborhood* and the friendly puppets of *Sesame Street* and *Eureeka's Castle*. [Nickelodeon] CEO Geraldine Laybourne says those models were "boring." She says Nick abandoned the idea of showing kids "really great role models to inspire them to go on and do great things for themselves." Instead the channel "enlisted kids in a conspiracy *against* the adult world." One early campaign told kids, "Send your parents to their room."[2]

While Nickelodeon does air some programs that support traditional family values, not coincidentally, those programs are almost always reruns of sixties and seventies shows. Contemporary parents, especially dads, are portrayed as bumbling fools, hopelessly confused, whose authority is constantly in question and whose intelligence quotient rivals that of a stone.

Meanwhile, Nickelodeon's older counterpart, MTV, pounds away at the psyches of America's teens. As one of the network's brazen slogans purported, "At MTV we don't shoot for the fourteen-year-olds, we own them." Much of the programming of MTV is offensive to parents.

What is a parent to do in the face of such direct opposition to your values? Most important of all, become aware of what your children are watching (or want to watch). Remember, it's okay to say no to certain programs that consistently violate the family values you are teaching your children. Monitor the cartoons, children's programs, and situation comedies that you do allow your children to watch. Change the channel when programs dishonor your established values. Be especially sensitive to the images portrayed of moms and dads, and the way children relate to them. When an inappropriate situation flashes onto the screen and catches you off guard, talk about what you have seen with your children, and explain why you disagree with the message being conveyed. If you do not have the time or the willingness to do that, you would be far better off to simply turn off the television. Do not depend on television programming to be a value-enhancing influence upon your family. Very few modern programs uphold the values we want to instill in our children.

Whatever you do, *please* do not allow the television to serve as your babysitter. If you allow your children to watch endless hours of unchallenged trash on the tube, you will soon see parallels in their conduct and hear the same sort of language used on television coming from the mouths of your children. Worse still, the values portrayed as normal on television will soon be instilled in your children's hearts and minds.

Movies, Music, and MTV
Running a close second in the race to indoctrinate your child is the influence of movies and music. This is especially true for older children, although do not let it slip by your attention that, financially speaking, some of the highest grossing movies in recent years have been children's movies. While it is worth applauding the film industry for making children's films, be sure to preview the message those movies are conveying to your child, or at least talk about the message after

you and your child have seen it. Also beware of the more sub-
tle themes and messages being presented. For example, an
August 5, 1996, press release from the American Family
Association included the following quote: "In *The Little
Mermaid,* a scene depicts a priest becoming noticeably aroused
while presiding over a wedding." Was this done by accident?
Or was there more to the message of the movie than most par-
ents caught?

Music has always been and always will be a point of contention between parents and children. The difference, of
course, is that much of modern music aimed at your child is
armed with messages that are contrary to many of the moral
values and virtues you are trying to teach your child. It is not
within the scope of this book to delve into what is acceptable
and what is obscene in the medium of music. Suffice it to say
that many song lyrics nowadays advocate violence, homosex-
ual practices, promiscuity, murder, suicide—all in the name of
free expression. If you think I am exaggerating the danger to
your child, I challenge you to stop by a store where today's
music is being sold. Ask to examine some of the lyrics, and
then you decide for yourself if you want those messages
impressed upon the mind of your child by multiple repetitions
with the help of a catchy beat. Remember, it is okay to say no
to destructive music. Plenty of fabulous music is being per-
formed and recorded nowadays. We have a virtual smorgas-
bord of great music available to us. How sad it would be to
allow your child to feast on garbage, when there is so much
good stuff out there.

Michael and Stormie Omartian are no strangers to the
power of music. Michael has won multiple Grammy Awards,
the music industry's highest accolade, and Stormie is an
award-winning singer and songwriter. Not surprisingly, when
the Omartians' son Christopher was fourteen, he became

enamored with musicians and covered his bedroom walls with posters of the musicians he admired most. Mom and Dad were not pleased. Stormie explains:

> The problem was that in some of the pictures the attire and the music being represented were offensive to his father and me and not glorifying to God. When we asked Christopher to take those particular posters down and explained why, he balked, then with a less than humble spirit did what we asked. A short time later, however, he replaced them with new ones which were just as bad. We again confronted him, took appropriate disciplinary measures, and this time we took them *all* down for him. Christopher was not happy, and we recognized we were dealing with the early manifestations of a rebellious spirit. . . . We prayed. . . . Our son's attitude changed, and the next time he put up posters they met the requirements we, as his parents, had established. This was the power of God in action, employed by praying parents.
>
> Wall posters seem like such a minor issue now, but at the time we were dealing with a strong will that was exalting itself over parents and God. And by resisting that display of rebellion, we were able to stop it before it became something major.[3]

If television, movies, and music have such a powerful impact on the values of your children, what happens when you put all three elements together in the form of a music video playing on MTV or some other video channel? You guessed it. Your children receive a one-two punch to their character. Again, it is time to say no when you realize that your children may be ingesting a steady diet of imagery that is counterproductive to nearly everything you believe to be right and good for them and your entire family.

Curfews

Another area in which you must muster enough courage to say no to your child is that of what time to be home. It is okay to say, "No, I do not want you out past midnight." Certainly, curfews may vary depending on your child's age, maturity level, what day of the week it is, whether there is school or church the next day, and other factors. Curfews, as I mentioned previously, are another way of simply letting your child know that you love them enough to set boundaries by which you expect them to abide.

When Reagan was fifteen years old, Tee and I gave her a cellular phone to carry with her so she could keep in touch when out with her friends. One night, Reagan called us three times from three different locations within an hour, simply to let us know where she was. Her friends were surprised. "Why do you keep calling home?" one of them asked.

Reagan replied, "Because my parents asked me to call if there was any change in my plans, so they would know what time to expect me home. What time did your parents tell you that you have to be in?"

"Oh, my parents never give me a curfew," one of the girls said.

Mom and Dad, what message are you sending to your children by failing to set a time to be home?

Granted, it is not always easy to say no to your children when they want to stay out later than you think is appropriate. In this respect, it becomes increasingly difficult to restrict your children as they get older. Nevertheless, the adage you probably heard from your parents is still a good one: "As long as you live under our roof, and put your feet under our table, you will abide by our house rules." One of your greatest allies will be your child's driver's license.

YOUR CHILD'S DRIVER'S LICENSE:
LIABILITY OR ASSET?

Your child's driver's license can be a tremendous tool in your discipline of that child. The automobile and the license to drive it give you leverage with your child that may not be there any other way. When your child balks at your instructions, it is not out of the question to say, "If you want to get your driver's license and drive a car, here are some things you must do to earn and keep that privilege. . . ."

Similarly, once your child has her license, use of the family vehicle can be used as a leverage point. "Since you are using the car, you must be home by eleven o'clock."

If your child has purchased her own car, you may have to approach it from a more businesslike point of view:

"Who buys the gas for this car?"

"Who pays for the auto insurance on this car?"

"Who pays for the tires?"

"Who pays for the servicing of this vehicle?"

If your child answers questions such as those above with the answer, "I do," face it; you are dealing with a child whose bags are nearly packed. She is practically an adult, living under your roof. That doesn't mean you cannot say no to her, but it does mean that your options are much more limited if the child disobeys or otherwise ignores your commands. At that point, the stance you have taken—"If you want to live in our home, you must obey our rules"—must be backed by definitive action if the child refuses to abide by the house rules.

Regardless of age, any child for whom you have legal responsibility must obey the laws of the land concerning use of the automobile. Any sign of speeding, reckless driving, or showing off with the auto must be met by you the parent with an absolute refusal to allow use of the car until the child is willing to comply with the law. You may want to rescind your child's license or at least limit access to a vehicle for a period of time. As with any discipline, the loss of freedom must be emphasized. Do not make the time period too long, however, or in all likelihood, you will not be able to make it stand. Better to have a severely felt loss of freedom for a week than an ineffective loss of freedom for a month.

Certainly, as your child matures, you should be saying yes to her requests more frequently. How else will your child learn to take responsibility?

When I was sixteen years of age and had received my driver's license, I asked my dad if I could take three other guys to Atlanta for the weekend. To my amazement, and much to my mother's consternation, Dad permitted me to go. "How else is he going to learn?" he asked my mom. Consequently, three buddies and I made the two-hour trip from Gadsden, Alabama, to the big city of Atlanta. My friends and I rented a hotel room, went to Six Flags Over Georgia, and had a great time. We returned in one piece, safe and sound. (Yes, I know that was during a different era!)

Maybe because of my dad's example, when my daughter was sixteen years old and asked to take our family's pontoon boat out on the river with a group of her friends, Tee and I consented. We had confidence that she would keep the rules, because she understood that the use of the boat was a privilege, not a right. Furthermore, we had confidence that we could say yes to Reagan because we had not been afraid to say no to her.

It is a great feeling to be able to say yes or no to your child as the circumstances require. Yes is always readily accepted; no is not always so well received. But when you have trouble getting your point across to your child, keep it simple. As country crooner Lorrie Morgan asked in a song, "What part of 'no' don't you understand?"

THE WINNER'S FOCUS

1. Why do you think many parents are reluctant to say no to their children?

2. Approximately what percentage of the time do you say yes to your child's requests? What are some areas in which that number could be increased and still maintain your values, thus giving more significance to the times when you must say no?

3. How do you usually handle situations in which you have more information than your child does about a potentially dangerous or compromising request your child has made?

4. Why is it important to suggest an alternative activity when you must refuse your child's request? Describe a situation in which creative alternatives would not be possible, and both you and your child will simply have to "bite the bullet." Make a list of good alternatives for the times you can offer them.

5. What is the difference between saying no to something and no to someone?

6. How can you use your child's driver's license and access to an automobile as incentives to make right choices?

7. A good gauge to determine your child's maturity is the percentage of yes answers you are able to give to her requests. More yes answers indicate a more mature child. What yes answers have you given lately, and how are they helping your child learn to take responsibility?

10

Children Listen with Their Eyes

RECENTLY MY IMMEDIATE FAMILY members and I spent an entire evening watching old family videotapes that we had recorded over the years. Tee, Reagan, Brodie, and I howled with laughter as we watched the videos depicting Little League baseball games, piano and dance recitals, birthdays, basketball games, and hundreds of other special family memories.. Other segments in the videos tugged at our heartstrings as we relived some special family moments. One of the videos was particularly interesting.

Someone (who will remain nameless) had been filming a family event at our home, had set the video camera down, and had forgotten to turn it off! From its perch on a chair in our family room, the camera went right on recording our family's unguarded moments. Every comment spoken could be clearly heard, every action was recorded, even though many of the movements were seen only from the waist down to the toes. For more than ten minutes, the camera continued to capture on tape our every word and movement. We were all surprised and embarrassed when we saw the candid tape, and a bit grateful that we had not said or done anything totally outlandish!

As I watched that silly recording, I couldn't help thinking about the "tapes" that are rolling in our homes every day. Each day, our children are watching and listening to us, sometimes when we least expect it. We cannot fool them. They know what we are really made of. We may be able to fool other adults, but we cannot fake doing the right thing in front of our children. They see and hear us in our unguarded moments as well as when we are on our best behavior. They know when we are being consistent and when we are not.

I was born and raised in northeast Alabama, and I live there to this day. Speed-limit signs are seemingly disregarded in my part of the country. Oh, they still stand along most stretches of our scenic state highways, but few people pay much attention to them. In Alabama, as in many other states, almost anyone who has a driver's license feels that he has a divine right to speed . . . me included.

Consequently, one of the most appreciated gifts you could buy for one of my friends was a radar detector, or as they are affectionately known in some places, "a fuzz-buster." It's a device that is placed on the dashboard or sun visor of your car that emits a signal when it picks up the beam of a police radar. Because nobody bought me one for Christmas or for my birthday, I went out and bought the best radar detector I could find and mounted it on the dashboard of my truck. I could race up the highway with little fear of getting a speeding ticket, because the radar detector alerted me to any police who might be clocking my speed.

Please understand, I have the greatest respect for the law of the land and for the officers sworn to uphold that law, but when it came to driving over the speed limit, well . . . that didn't even seem like it was breaking the law. After all, most everybody I know drives faster than the speed limit.

When we were driving down the road one day, Brodie asked me, "Dad, do you obey the law?"

"Why, of course, Brodie. You know I would never do anything illegal."

"Oh, I know, Dad, but aren't you supposed to drive at or under the speed limit?"

"Yes, Brodie, that's exactly right. On this interstate highway, the speed limit is sixty-five miles per hour." I glanced down at my speedometer. I quickly eased my foot off the gas a bit.

"Well, if we are not supposed to go faster than the speed limit, why do we need that radar detector on the dashboard?"

My boy's searing words hit the bull's-eye. He was right. What he saw me doing negated all my fine words and principles about obeying the law. By placing that radar detector on my dash, I was announcing to all passengers, and to anyone else who saw my truck, that I fully intended to break the law. I was just going to take precautions to avoid getting caught. The message my boy was picking up on his internal "radar detector" was: "It's okay to break the law, as long as you don't get caught." I realized that I was compromising my integrity with my son for the sake of a few miles per hour.

I removed that radar detector and have never put it back on my dashboard.

YOUR CHILD REMEMBERS YOUR PROMISES

Not only do our children pick up on any inconsistencies in our actions, they also are quick to notice what is really important to us. This is especially true if you give any reason for your children to think that things such as money, prestige, power, position, or your job are higher priorities to you than they are. If you make a promise that you are going to be "there" for them, and then you allow something or someone else to take precedence over your promise, your children will not be pacified by weak excuses or promises of future times together. Whether you realize it or not, when you promise something to your child, it is a firm deal.

Have you ever heard comments such as these?

- "Daddy, you promised that you were going to play a game with me."
- "Mom, you said that after supper, we were going to take a walk."
- "Dad, I thought you were going to make it to my game tonight. We only have two games left this season."
- "Mom, you said you would read a story to me after lunch."
- "Dad, you promised that you would be home in time to go to the ball game with me."
- "Mom, why doesn't Daddy ever come to any of my recitals?"

In the movie *Hook*, a contemporary version of *Peter Pan*, the Pan character was known as Peter Banning, a successful but overworked and overstressed businessman. He always had a mobile flip phone in his hand. Peter's work always seemed to take precedence over his parenting responsibilities. Peter's intentions were good, he just had a hard time making it to his children's games and school functions.

Unfortunately, when Peter's children were kidnapped by the mean, nasty Captain Hook, Captain Hook was able to win over Peter's children by pretending to take an interest in their games and making a big deal out of attending them. Furthermore, Hook threw Peter's inconsistencies into the faces of his children as proof that he did not love them, no matter how hard he was working to provide for them. "Your father does not love you. Remember? He promised to be at your ball game, but he didn't show up. How could he be a loving father?" Regardless of Peter's excuses, Hook's arguments seared into the hearts and minds of Peter's children and, for a while, caused them to question their dad's love for them and their place on his priority list. In the movie, Peter nearly lost his children because he had not kept his promises to "be there" for them. Fortunately, Peter came through in the end, and everyone presumably lived happily ever after.

Your life, however, is not a movie, and you have no guarantee that everyone is going to live happily ever after unless you do what is right and keep your promises. Mom and Dad, I cannot overemphasize this point: Your children take your promises seriously!

We once had a little boy at Big Oak Ranch whose real father had arranged with us to come and pick up his child to spend the weekend with him. It is not our normal policy to arrange such visits—usually there is no request that we do so—but in the case of this little boy, we thought it might be helpful. His dad had promised the little boy that on Friday evening, after work, he would come to pick up the child at the Ranch.

On Friday afternoon, the boy hurried straight home after school. He didn't stop to play with any of the other children at the Ranch. Instead, he went directly into his home and up to his bedroom, where he changed his clothes. At about 3:30 P.M. the boy went back downstairs and sat down at the windowsill, so he could watch for his dad. At suppertime, he declined to join the rest of his Ranch family because he said his dad was coming and they were going out for pizza. The little boy stayed right by the window, waiting.

Soon darkness began to fall, but the boy remained steadfastly at the window. Each time we checked on him, he assured us his dad would be there any minute. Looking into the darkness, the little boy finally cried himself to sleep, sitting at the windowsill, where he had been watching and waiting for his daddy.

His dad never showed up.

I picked up the child, and as I was carrying him to his bedroom, he reached his arms around my neck and half-opened his sleep-heavy eyes long enough to say, "Is that you, Dad?"

Is that *you*, Dad? Is that *you*, Mom? Are you the parent who hasn't kept your promises to your children? You cannot continually emotionally stab somebody and say, "Oh, my! I am so sorry. Here, let me put a bandage over your wound," and then a few days later, do the same thing. Don't think they haven't noticed. Even if they have not said a word to you about it, you can be certain your children remember your broken promises. If you are not careful, and if you do not reverse that trend, it will not be long before your children lose confidence in your word.

Before you make a promise to your child, stop and ask yourself, *Can I really keep this promise?* Do not make a promise that you cannot keep. Do not make a promise that your responsibilities or the dictates of someone else will likely cause you to break. For example, Bill told his son Tommy, "If I don't have to work on Saturday, I will be at your ball game." Bill already knew that earlier that week, his boss had said to him, "Bill, I may need you to work on Saturday morning." That dad was setting himself up to disappoint his child.

On the other hand, I heard a story where a man named

Bob made a promise to his little girl, Caitlin. "Sweetheart, I will be at your birthday party on Tuesday afternoon. I have made arrangements to get off work early, and I will be home in time for the party. As a matter of fact, we are going to have some special games, and I will dress up as a clown to help entertain the children at the party."

Caitlin was ecstatic! "Oh, Daddy! Do you mean it? Really? You will be here? And you will dress up as the clown?"

"That's right, darling. I wouldn't miss it for the world."

On Monday of the following week, Bob's boss announced a special emergency board meeting at work . . . to be held Tuesday afternoon. Immediately, Bob went in to see his boss to check on the possibility of missing the meeting.

"Out of the question," Bob's boss told him. "Bob, I need you at that meeting Tuesday afternoon. It is very important."

Bob left his boss's office discouraged and disappointed. How would he ever explain this to Caitlin?

That evening when he got home, he gathered his wife and daughter around him and tried to explain the situation at work. "Sweetheart, something has come up and Daddy has to attend the board meeting. I am really sorry. I will do my best to make it up to you."

With tears filling her eyes, Caitlin asked, "But Daddy, who will be the clown?"

The next morning Bob went in to work and headed straight for the boss's office. "Tell me about this special board meeting this afternoon. What's going on?" Bob asked. The boss explained the important matters to be addressed at the meeting. Bob listened intently and offered a few suggestions as the boss outlined the agenda for the meeting. When the boss finally finished describing what needed to be done at the meeting, Bob took a deep breath and said, "Well, I'm sorry, but I can't be at the meeting this afternoon."

"What?" the boss roared. "What could you possibly have to do today that is more important than this meeting?"

Without blinking, Bob replied, "I am going home to be a clown. "

Not everyone has an employment situation that would allow him or her to simply walk off the job and go home to his or her family. Nor does everyone have the luxury of being able to make such a bold statement to his or her boss. But Bob was confident in his position at work. And he knew that he would be a better employee at work because of keeping his promise at home.

BALANCING PRIORITIES WITH RESPONSIBILITIES

Most parents want to give their children the proper place on their priority lists, but it is not always easy to do so. You have responsibilities to your employer, the community, the government, and your church. All sorts of other people are tugging at you, wanting a piece of your time. How can you possibly balance the priorities in your life with the many responsibilities you have?

For instance, let's say you are on the governing board of your church. Your church board meeting begins at 5:30 P.M. and your son has a ball game at 7:00. What are you going to do?

I can't answer for you, but if I were facing a similar dilemma (which I often do), I can tell you what I would do. At 6:45 P.M. I would say, "As I mentioned earlier, you folks will have to excuse me, but I must leave our meeting early tonight. My son has a ball game, and I promised him I would be there. That is my top priority this evening."

I heard not too long ago of a dad who worked out an arrangement with his boss whereby the dad could go in to work an hour early so he could leave an hour early on those days when his son had a ball game. The dad was willing to sacrifice and do whatever was necessary, even if it meant going out of his way to meet his work responsibilities to show his son that he was a priority. (This also showed respect to his boss.)

My dad had plenty of responsibilities as I was growing up, but he always showed me by his actions that I was one of his top priorities. Throughout my life, Dad was always in the grandstands for me, cheering me on whether I was playing in a Little League game, a high school basketball game, or a college football game competing for a national championship. I couldn't always see him in the crowd, but I knew my dad was there for me. Throughout my athletic career, my dad missed only two games.

Although Dad never told me, I later found out that when I was in ninth grade, my dad turned down an opportunity in another city which would have been a tremendous career advancement and give him an increase in salary. Dad declined the position so I could remain in the highly touted athletic program in the Gadsden school system where I was already being noticed by college scouts.

When I was in high school, Dad told his boss, "I will work Thursday nights and I will work Saturdays if you want me to, but I will not work on Friday nights because I want to be at my son's ball games." The boss consented to Dad's proposal.

Granted, some occupations do not lend themselves to accommodating a child's extracurricular activities. In such cases, you must sit down with your child and do your best to explain the circumstances in advance. "Sweetheart, you know I can't leave work early, so I am going to miss the first part of your piano recital. I want you to know, though, that I will be there for the second half." You had better be there!

Most children can accept something like that. And their eyes will light up the moment you show up. But if you repeatedly promise to show and do not, you will extinguish much more than the light in your child's eyes. You will snuff out the fire in her heart.

Frankly, for some parents it is impossible for them to attend some of the events in which their children are participating, no matter how hard the parents try to shuffle their schedules, or how much they are willing to work unusual hours. In these cases, personal rather than professional sacrifice is required. For instance, imagine that you are a traveling salesperson who misses the special events in your child's life every week, Monday through Friday. When you are home on the weekend, your child must be a high priority, with only God and your spouse coming before him. Of course it would be easy for you to say, "Hey, I have been gone all week long. I have had a rough time of things out there on the road. I need some time for myself, just to unwind. I think I'll book a round of golf on Saturday and afterward, if there is still time, I can stop by to watch my son's baseball game."

That would be a clear example of having your priorities upside down. Rather than unwinding on the golf course, you need to unwind in the grandstands, while you are cheering on your son.

Certainly, in all of our lives there are times when our best-laid plans are pulverized by someone else's demands on our time. You need not feel guilty for that. But when those situations occur, do your best to explain to your child why you have had to break a promise. Avoid allowing outside influences to repeatedly dictate your schedule with your family. Sometimes situations arise that are out of your control, but this excuse can only be used a certain number of times before your child begins to feel that you are passing off this excuse as a reason. If you have any choice at all in the matter, do not break a promise to your child. Although you may have many responsibilities—and I have met few productive people who do not have a plateful of them—you must show your child again and again that he is at the top of your priority list.

Mark this: Your child may not always remember all the games (plays, recitals, music programs) that you attended, but he will never forget the ones you missed.

HOW TO DETERMINE PRIORITIES
VERSUS RESPONSIBILITIES

The longer I work with children, the more convinced I am that there is no such thing as accidental parenting. You don't happen to be a parent; you don't simply parent your children when it is fun, interesting, or convenient. Similarly, your children will not receive positive parenting by osmosis. You have to be actively involved with your children if you hope to have a positive influence upon them. That takes time, and that means you are going to be constantly faced with decisions about what is really important in your life. How will you make those decisions between priorities and responsibilities? How can you tell the difference?

Four questions help my staff and me to clarify what is important around Big Oak Ranch and for our families. We ask ourselves these questions for both large and small decisions, though not all situations require all four questions before the priority is realized. When you must determine the priorities and responsibilities in your life, ask yourself:

1. Is what I am doing (or what I am considering doing) what God wants me to do? Do I sense a higher calling to do this beyond mere monetary gain or ego gratification?
2. Is this what I can do best?
3. Is this what brings me the most joy and happiness?
4. Is this what I would do if I had only one year to live?

When deciding whether something is really important in your life, if you cannot answer yes to all four questions, you should stop and reevaluate. What you are considering may be a responsibility or an opportunity for you, but it may not be a priority at this time. Perhaps that will change later, but until you can honestly answer yes to all four questions, move that choice down lower on the totem pole of your priorities.

They Gotta Know You Will Be There for Them

Our children need to know that to the best of our abilities, we will be there for them when they need us. If we can instill within our children the confidence that we will never give up on them, they can make it through the deepest trials of life. The true story of a young girl named Sherry confirms this truth.

Sherry was riding with her younger brother on the front of the family pontoon boat as her father steered it down the river. It was a beautiful day and everyone was enjoying the weather and scenery. The river was perfectly calm when, suddenly, they hit a patch of rough, turbulent water. The boat's motor sputtered and then jolted to a stop. The father didn't understand what had stopped the boat as the water was again relatively calm. He glanced over the stern to see what was wrong with the engine.

As he looked into the water around the rear of the pontoon, he saw that the propeller blades were tangled in some familiar-looking red fabric. Gripped with fear, the father whirled around and quickly searched the bow of the boat with his eyes.

His son, who was now standing on the front of the pontoon, was heaving his shoulders, gulping for air. He pointed beneath the boat. "Sherry fell in!" he managed to say.

The father peered into the water. What he saw froze his heart. There, just barely a foot beneath the surface, was his little girl, holding her breath. Her eyes were wide open as she looked up through the ripples at her father. Miraculously, though, she was not panic-stricken, and she continued holding her breath.

Immediately the dad dived into the water. As he reached her, his daughter was still calmly holding her breath, her eyes locked on him. He struggled for what seemed like minutes to free her red sweater from the propeller blades, but he was unsuccessful. He yanked and pulled and stretched the sweater every way possible, but try as he might, he could not free Sherry.

The dad was getting desperate; he didn't know what to do! Yet all this time, Sherry never took her eyes off him. She calmly continued to watch him, still holding her breath.

Realizing that Sherry would soon be out of air, the father went back to the surface and filled his lungs with air. He dived back down to the propeller, and covering his daughter's mouth with his, he blew life-giving air into her lungs. With increasing desperation he tugged at the sweater, still to no avail.

Again he surfaced for air. This time as he broke the plane of the water, the father saw his young son standing over him. "Here, Dad!" he called. "Take this knife!"

Grabbing the old, dull knife from his son and again filling his lungs, the father dived back down to free his daughter. Working quickly, he finally managed to cut her loose. He pulled her to the surface where she gasped for air.

Miraculously, she seemed to have suffered only minor cuts and bruises from the motor. But the father was taking no chances; he rushed her to the hospital. There, one of the astonished members of the medical staff asked the little girl how she had been able to maintain her composure through the terrifying ordeal.

"Well," she said, "we live near the water, and my father always taught me not to panic when there was danger." She paused for a second as she looked at her father. "Besides, I knew my daddy would come get me."

Sherry knew that if it were humanly possible, her dad would be there for her, just when she needed him the most. Dad, Mom, do your children know that about you? That you will always be there for them? That you will never give up trying to help them, working to bring out the winners in them, no matter what the cost to you personally?

Every day our children meet obstacles and dangers just as serious as those Sherry faced when she encountered the churning propellers under water. Every day our children will have to make decisions on how to handle the challenges in their lives, from inconveniences such as having a flat tire, to devastating blows such as losing a job, to tragedies such as divorce or the death of a loved one. If we can teach our children not to panic when they encounter difficulty, if we can teach them to be confident in the values and habits and lessons we have instilled in them, then we will have been successful in our role as parents.

The harsh realities of life will not go away. We may experience a lag between tough times, but they inevitably come to all of us in one form or another. As I reflect on the incredible courage of young Sherry, I am convinced that the most important factor in that little girl's survival was the knowledge—no, the unshakable conviction—that her father would come to save her.

We may not know what kind of house Sherry lived in, or what kind of clothes her parents bought for her, or what kind of car her mom or dad drove her to school in, but we have absolutely no doubt that her mom and dad endowed her with great character.

Do your children have this same legacy?

Johnny Musso was an incredible running back and one of my teammates on the football team at the University of Alabama. I could probably fill a book with nothing but classic Musso stories. The incident that I remember best about Johnny Musso did not occur on the football field. It happened at Johnny's home, at a dinner party, years after we had both hung up our cleats.

Johnny's home was packed with dignitaries that evening, famous celebrities, political powerhouses, and the sort—I mean "big dog" celebrities. Johnny was the consummate host, moving from one conversation to the next, making sure everyone was comfortable and enjoying the party.

At one point in the evening, Johnny Musso's little boy suddenly came running through the hallway and down the steps, calling out, "Dad! Dad! Dad!" Johnny stopped in his tracks and knelt down to meet his son as the boy cleared the last step. The boy stopped only six inches from Johnny's face. "Dad," he said excitedly, "I just wanted to tell you that I am getting ready to go to bed, and I just wanted to tell you good night."

Johnny stood to his feet, turned to his dignified guests, and said, "Please excuse me for a minute."

He got back down with his son, kissed him and hugged him, and for a long moment nobody else existed in that house to Johnny but his boy. Johnny picked up his son and went upstairs to tuck him into bed.

Johnny Musso's actions had a lasting impact upon my life. Johnny was showing all of us in the house that night what it means to be a great parent. Beyond that, he was showing his son that he was a priority in his life.

Repeatable Blessings,
Unforgettable Memories

Since they were infants, before my two children went to bed, Tee and I hugged their necks and kissed them. To this day, we tell them that we love them; they tell us that they love us and we pray together. If I am staying overnight away from home, traveling for a speaking engagement or some other purpose, I will call home and try to spend a few minutes at the close of the day with the children and Tee. Besides bringing closure to each day, this little repeatable blessing bonds us together as a family. Should some awful tragedy ever befall me, I want the memories of our nights together with our children to be us hugging each other, kissing each other, and praying together.

This reminds me of a story I heard some time ago: A doctor, his son, and two other men flew to a fishing site in the northern part of the United States. On their way back, the plane's engine died, and the small aircraft plunged into the sea. All of the passengers survived the crash, but they were stranded in the chilly waters of the North Atlantic Ocean . . . and the tide was going out. Frantically, the two men started swimming toward shore. The doctor found his boy in the wreckage and struggled together with him toward the shore. The two other men were strong enough to make it, but the cold waters quickly began to take a toll upon the boy.

When the two men finally got to shore, they turned around to look for the doctor and his son. There amid the whitecaps were father and son. With one hand, the father waved to his friends and with the other he held on to his son . . . as the waves swept them out to sea.

Mom and Dad, does your child know that you will never willingly let him down, that you will not let go or give up on him, even if it costs your life? Does your child know that no matter who else turns his back on him, you will hold on till the end?

All of your pretty-sounding words are useless unless your children can see from your actions that they are the priority in your life. Remember, children listen with their eyes.

THE WINNER'S FOCUS

1. If someone with a concealed camera were to spend some time in your home, what words or actions of yours toward your children would they catch on tape? Would the tape be an encouragement to you or an embarrassment?

2. In what ways are you showing your children that they are a priority in your life? In what ways are you showing them they are not a priority?

3. What promises have you made to your child that you have not kept? What can you do to possibly keep one of those promises yet?

4. What changes can you make in your schedule that will allow you to attend more of your child's activities?

11

Quality Time
Never Comes

O NE DAY WHEN I was about ten years old, I came running into the house carrying a baseball and glove and calling out to my father, "Come on, Dad. Let's go play pitch!" Dad didn't look too excited about the idea, but he consented anyway. He pulled a chair outside in the yard and sat down in it. I tossed him the ball, and Dad rolled the ball back to me. I threw another pitch into his mitt, and Dad returned the ball to me.

"What's wrong, Dad? Are you okay?" I asked. Dad was usually energetic when it came to playing ball with me. On this day, he seemed to be just going through the motions.

"Oh, I'm fine," Dad replied. "Just a little tired, I guess."

We had played for about five minutes when Dad said, "John, I can't play anymore right now. I need to go back inside the house."

I thought my dad's actions were highly unusual. Dad struggled back into the house where he lay down on the couch for the remainder of the day.

Later that afternoon when my mom got home, I told her, "Dad played pitch with me this morning, but he sure was acting strange."

Mom stopped what she was doing and said, "Your dad did what?"

"He played pitch—you know, pitching and catching the ball. But he didn't do too well. And he quit after only a few minutes. He was no fun."

"John," Mom said seriously, "your dad has strep throat and a temperature of 104 degrees. He should be in bed. Do you mean to tell me he played pitch with you?"

"Yes, ma'am, he did."

Years later, I asked my dad why he played ball with me that day when he was so sick. Dad replied, "When you were still in your crib, I made you a promise that if you ever asked me to play with you, I would never tell you no. All my life, my daddy never once played pitch with me. Nor did he ever come to my ball games, except maybe one time. And I really wished that he had. So I made a vow to you, that whenever you asked me to play, I would never turn you down."

My family was not wealthy. My mom and dad worked hard to make ends meet. My parents were not able to give me expensive gifts, but they gave me something far more precious—their time.

Children Spell Love T-I-M-E

Practically speaking, if you are going to help bring out the winner in your child, it is going to take time. Tons of time! Love always takes time.

Nowadays, we hear a great deal of discussion about *quality* time versus *quantity* of time. We should not make it necessary for our children to distinguish between the two. After all, when was the last time you heard an eight-year-old say, "Well, Dad could spend only five minutes with me today, but hmmm-hmm, it was *quality* time!"

Get real! Our children do not make such silly distinctions. Frankly, I have found that the most adamant advocates of *quality* time over *quantity* of time usually aren't giving much of either, and their philosophical gibberish is merely a futile attempt to excuse the fact that they know they are failing their children. Quality time is the result of investing quantities of time with your children. You cannot pick quality time. You cannot pull your six-year-old child into your lap and say, "I have ten minutes. We will now have quality time." Believe me, you do not pick the moment for quality time. Parenting takes time!

It's not easy to spend enough time with your child. This is especially true if you are a single parent, or if you have been through a divorce and because of custody rights and visitation privileges you have only limited access to your child. A famous man came to visit us at Big Oak Ranch. At the time, the man and his wife had recently been embroiled in a nasty divorce settlement, and the father was trying desperately to maintain a good relationship with his six-year-old son. As I showed the man around the Ranch, he was telling me all the things he was going to do with his boy: "We're going to go here; we're going there; we'll do this or that. I'm going to give my boy this gift or that. . . ."

Finally, I said, "Stop! Wait a minute. I really think that is the wrong approach."

This man was shocked. "What do you mean?" he asked.

"Here's what you need to do," I said. "Take your son, saddle up two horses, put some food in a backpack, take two sleeping bags, and the two of you go out in the woods and spend some real time together. Build a fire and cook some hot dogs for supper. Then when it is time to go to sleep, snuggle up with your little boy in a sleeping bag, and look up at the stars. Tell your boy, 'There is a God way up there, and He gave you to your mama and me. And I just want to be sure you know that I love you, and you are my most prized gift. I am your daddy, and I will always love you, no matter what.' Then when your boy goes back home to live with his mother, if anyone ever says to him, 'Your daddy doesn't really love you,' that boy can say, 'Oh, yes, he does. He told me so, and I have experienced it.'"

It takes time, creativity, and commitment to be a good parent, especially if you are trying to raise a child by yourself. But it can be done.

One word of caution, though: You can't be a "Disneyland Parent." By that I mean that you cannot spend a few hours a week with your child doing all the fun things, going to amusement parks, concerts, or games, showering your child with gifts, toys, and trinkets, while your mate (or former mate) is the disciplinarian who makes the child toe the line, do his homework and chores around the house, and oversees all the other mundane items in the child's daily routine. Naturally, the child will gravitate toward the Disneyland Parent for a while. But when he realizes what you have been doing— trying to buy him off—he will resent you. The Disneyland Parent always loses in the end.

Besides, your child doesn't want *things.* Your child wants *you!*

Often parents are fooled into thinking, *The best thing I can do for my children is to go out and make a good living so I can provide them with all the things that I never had as I was growing up.* As I said before, sometimes we get so busy trying to give our children all the things we did not have that we neglect to give them the things we did have—things such as values and virtues, unconditional love, unhurried time, and our undivided attention.

Besides, your children don't care about what you do. They are much more concerned with what you are. What you are will determine what you do, not only what you do for a living, but what you do in every season of life.

Stop and think: Is pouring so much of your precious, limited time and energy into maintaining your lifestyle really a good investment compared to the short window of time you have with your children? How much of the material possessions that you spend your life trying to obtain will be worth anything a hundred years from now? How about twenty years from now? On the other hand, your relationship with your children will last forever.

BE A PRESENT PARENT

Our children do not expect us to be perfect parents, but they do expect us to be present parents. A friend of mine is a well-known professional football player. He makes a lot of money and buys all sorts of gifts for his children. Unfortunately, he is away from home so much that he rarely spends enough time with his children. At one point, he was gone for seven straight weeks, during which he did not see his children. Once he and I were talking about that subject, and I said, "I guarantee you that if your children had a choice between having all those expensive gifts and having you home more often, they would choose you."

With one of the saddest expressions I have ever seen, the highly successful pro football player replied softly, "I don't think so."

What a tragedy! He thought his children would rather have material things than their daddy. His story is not the norm; as I mentioned above, most children would choose their parent over the most expensive present. Yet, unfortunately, his was a self-fulfilling prophecy, a monster he had created himself by his naive idea that his presents could somehow substitute for his presence in his children's lives. Was his Super Bowl ring worth the loss of his children?

At times it has been my difficult duty to visit the bedside of a dying patient. Not once have I ever heard a busy businessman or a successful career woman say, "I wish I had spent more time at the office." On numerous occasions I have heard words similar to this: "My biggest regret is that I did not spend more time with my family." Don't make that same mistake. Your time may be the greatest gift you ever give to your children. And it is the one gift they can't break!

Admittedly, you may not always be able to give your children an abundance of time, but when you are with them, you must give your undivided attention. Your child should not have to compete with the newspaper, a magazine, a computer modem, or the television remote control.

A daddy was watching his children play in the back yard. The children did not know that their daddy was watching and listening to them. The dad's chest swelled with pride when he heard one of his children say, "It's your turn to play the daddy." But his youngest daughter quickly burst his bubble when she said, "I don't want to be the daddy, because all the daddy does is play with the remote control." Sound familiar?

YOUR CHILD KNOWS
WHAT IS IMPORTANT TO YOU

Your children know what is really important to you by the amount of time you put into each activity. Zig Ziglar notes:

> The parent who watches several hours of television a
> day but doesn't have time to take the child to the soccer

match clearly communicates to the child that watching television is a much higher priority than spending time with them, watching them grow and develop. The father who spends ten hours a week on the golf course but doesn't have time to take his family to dinner is clearly communicating what his priorities are and where his family ranks on the totem pole of importance. The father who buys expensive sports equipment and has time to go hunting and fishing but does not have time to take his children to Sunday school and church, because it's the "only day I have for myself," is clearly saying that the importance of teaching spiritual values and honoring God is a distant second to his own personal indulgences.[1]

The truth is, if you are too busy to train your children, you are still training them—by your poor example. Automaker Henry Ford often said, "You can't build a reputation on what you are going to do." Similarly, you cannot begin working to bring out the winner in your child "one of these days." *You must start now.* If that means shuffling your schedule so you can spend more time with your children, do it, if at all possible. It will be worth it in the long run. I guarantee it.

Sure you are busy. We are all busy. Most people who are doing something productive with their lives are busy. In fact, I never ask an idle man or woman to help me with a project. I ask people who are "shakin' and bakin'" to make things happen. They are successful because their priorities are in correct alignment; they have discovered the secret to getting more done with the same twenty-four hours that everyone else has. Isn't it amazing, then, how we always seem to find the time for what we really want to do?

Susanna Wesley is best known as the mother of John and Charles Wesley. John founded the Methodist Church, and Charles was a great hymn-writer who gave us such classic music as "Hark! The Herald Angels Sing!" and "Oh, For a Thousand Tongues." But John and Charles were only two of Susanna's *nineteen* children, so Susanna, a busy mom to say the least, committed herself to spending a minimum of one hour a week with each child, giving that child her exclusive, undivided attention during that time. Granted, she did not have car-pool duty, but neither did she have a washing machine, microwave oven, or a pager. Yet this woman who was dedicated to training her children found a way to do it.

A popular slogan on T-shirts nowadays is *Carpe Diem,* which is Latin for "Seize the day." In other words, do all you can to take advantage of the opportunities this day affords. Nowhere is *Carpe Diem* more appropriate than in the area of parenting your children. You must seize every opportunity you have to train your children, but also to enjoy just being with them. You will not have that opportunity for long.

Carpe Diem. Seize the day. Don't miss out on an opportunity to watch your child's eyes light up.

Practical Ways You Can
Seize the Day with Your Child

It doesn't necessarily cost a lot of money or require you to go someplace special with your child to make special memories of time spent together. When Brodie was younger, a couple of times a week, I used to come home to eat lunch with him instead of eating at the office or going out to a restaurant for lunch. It was a simple thing, something I was able to do because my office is close to our home, but what a memory—for both of us!

Brodie and I have done many wonderful and exciting

things together. We played golf together in New York. We rode horses in the desert in Arizona. We went deer hunting together at exclusive, private hunting clubs. Once I asked Brodie what he thought was the most enjoyable thing we had ever done together. I was expecting Brodie to name some far-away place we had visited or some big ball game we had attended or some prestigious event we were honored to be a part of. Instead, without a moment of hesitation, Brodie fielded my question and tossed me an answer. "Trail rides," he replied matter-of-factly, "when it was just you and me."

Trail rides? I thought to myself. *What is so special about a trail ride? That's something we could do almost any time we wanted. After all, we live on a ranch!* Granted, riding a beautiful horse through the hills of Alabama is a treat that I never want to take for granted, and for you, especially if you live in the midst of a major metropolitan center, a trail ride might be a fascinating and relaxing experience. But for us, where we live, trail rides are not that exotic.

It did not matter to my child that we do something fancy or expensive or far off. It only mattered to my boy that he and his dad were able to saddle up two horses and go off on a leisurely ride through the woods—together. Sometimes when Brodie and I went out in the woods, Tee packed us some hot dogs, and Brodie and I would build a small fire. It did not cost a lot of money, but, oh, what an investment that time was! I did the same thing with Reagan when she was younger.

One of the best times Reagan, Brodie, Tee, and I ever had together was when the children were young. We went hiking in the woods and played hide-and-seek for more than an hour. There we were, my wife and I hiding in a tree from our children. Brodie came along, stopped right below the tree in which we were hiding, then turned and casually looked up at us and said, "Gotcha!"

It doesn't cost any money to play hide-and-seek, or to play tag, or to take a walk in a park. It just takes some time, and the desire to do it.

WHAT ABOUT MY MATE?

It is easy to become so consumed with trying to bring out the winner in your child and spending the necessary time it takes to do so that you neglect to meet the needs of the winner to whom you are married. One mother of three children under ten years of age expressed it well: "After I chase three children around all day, preparing their meals, getting their clothes ready, running them here and there across town for doctor's appointments, music lessons, and all the rest, I barely have enough energy left to stand up by the time my husband comes home. I couldn't care less about meeting his needs, or frankly, about his meeting mine. At that point, every cell in my body is simply screaming, 'Take me away!'"

I know a lot of parents who can relate to that woman's lament. Sometimes the only encouragement we can offer to those forging through the chaos of raising children is, "This too will pass." No question about it. It's tough being both a spouse and a parent. Ideally, however, we are meant to be marriage partners before we are parents, and that order should be maintained. In other words, you are working against the grain when you consistently put your child ahead of your mate. In fact, the best way you can show love to your children is by loving your marriage partner. Your children will catch on quickly, when they see and hear you honoring and respecting your mate, and they will do the same. That is the good news.

The bad news is that they will also notice if there is any animosity between you and your mate. If you treat your marriage partner disrespectfully or speak to him or her using foul language or a mean tone of voice, your children will do the same. Furthermore, your child will carry the same concepts of marriage he observes in you and your mate—both the positive and the negative ways you and your spouse relate to each other as husband and wife—into his own relationship with his future marriage partner.

How do Tee and I keep a balance in our relationship with each other and with our children while being responsible for almost one hundred children at any given time?

Sometimes not very well.

Does that surprise you? The truth is, we have to work at our relationship just as you do yours. At times I have been a terrible husband. And as I have already alluded to previously, I have made many mistakes. I have learned through those mistakes, however. If we do not learn from our mistakes, we are destined to repeat them, and some of my mistakes were too painful to go through again.

It takes a long time to bring balance to a relationship. In the past I have chosen the kids or other people, things, or duties ahead of my wife. I've even allowed my own insecurities and selfishness to stand in the way. But there came a time in my life when I drew a line in the sand and said "Never again!"

Consequently, I now work even harder at balancing my relationship with Tee and my relationship with Reagan and Brodie. Because Tee shares my passion to see our children turn into champions, sometimes she makes my job almost too easy. For example, when our twentieth wedding anniversary was approaching, I saved money for months and months, hoping to somehow take Tee on a romantic Caribbean cruise. As the date drew nearer, Tee and I were looking at brochures and making choices about various destinations and cabin selections and all. Tee looked across the table at me and said, "John, where would you rather be on our twentieth anniversary? On a ship with a bunch of people we don't even know, or with our children?"

"With our children," I replied.

"Me too," said Tee.

That was the end of our cruise plans. We celebrated our twentieth anniversary by cooking some steaks and having a special picnic dinner in our family den with our two children.

No doubt, some marriage and family counselors might criticize us for our decision, but it was not one parent choosing the children over the other. Nor were we putting our children ahead of our marriage relationship. Both Tee and I wanted to include our children in the celebration. Moreover, our children recognized that we had the chance to go away without them for the special event, but instead we chose to be with them. Someday that choice alone will speak volumes to Reagan and Brodie.

Certainly every married couple needs time alone, away from the children, and I would encourage you to take that. Again, it doesn't have to be glitzy or glamorous, although most couples occasionally enjoy adding a bit of adventure and spice to their everyday relationship. Many times all you need to do is look at your mate and say, "Honey, you have had a tough week. Let's call a babysitter and go out for dinner alone on Saturday night."

At other times, you may choose to include the children. Keep them guessing. One hot summer afternoon, George called his wife, Angela, at 1:00 P.M. and said, "Honey, don't cook supper tonight. Gather the children and meet me at the big picnic pavilion at the lake this afternoon around 4:00 P.M."

"What?" Angela protested. "What's going on?"

"Just be there," said George with a mischievous tone in his voice. "Oh, and don't you and the kids forget to wear your swimming suits."

That afternoon, when the family arrived at the lake, George was already there. He had rented Jet-skis for the entire family. For nearly two hours, they had a blast racing the Jet-skis across the lake.

Just about 6:00 P.M. a pizza delivery truck pulled in to the parking area near the pavilion. The delivery man brought over the pizzas George had ordered in advance. As the family sat at the picnic tables, eating pizza, laughing and having a great time, Angela was happy because she didn't have to cook on such a warm evening, the children were happy because of the fun they were having, and George was delighted at the special memory they were making as a family. The entire event had not cost George a lot of money, just a bit of creativity and the willingness to invest some time in his family.

TAKE YOUR CHILD TO WORK

Your schedule may be such that there is little time left in your day to squeeze in special trips to the lake. Don't despair. If you look hard enough, you will find a way to spend time with your children. One woman I know makes her living cleaning houses for other families. She is a single parent, and she cannot afford a babysitter, so she takes her four-year-old daughter to work with her. The daughter even helps with small chores as the mom is making a living.

Obviously, not all occupations lend themselves to your children accompanying you, but the idea of occasionally taking one or all of them to work with you is a good one. Most bosses, nowadays, would welcome some such involvement on the part of their employees. Many companies actually sponsor events in which you can take your son or daughter into the workplace.

Besides exposing your children to a better understanding of future career opportunities, acquainting them with your workplace provides a better understanding of what you do and why you cannot always be home, or why you must at times miss certain events.

Another way to spend time with your children while working is to take them with you while you serve in community involvement projects. Volunteer to serve with your local hospital auxiliary, or in your local library or food bank, or in a homeless shelter serving a Thanksgiving dinner. When you do, take your kids with you. Your children will gain invaluable experience as you open their eyes to the world they live in, while contributing to the community, learning about serving others, all while having a good time with you, their parents.

Regardless of how much or how little time you have to spend with your children, make the most of it. If you work at home, as more and more people do, take frequent breaks to spend a few minutes with each of your children. You will be refreshed when you return to your work, and your children will not feel deprived because you are at home but cannot spend the total time with them.

For the parent who says, "Well, I don't have time to do all those things with my child," let me remind you that you have your children for only a short period of time, and you don't get a second chance to enjoy their childhood with them. Beyond that, if you fail to take time with your children, a day will come when they will no longer want to spend time with you. Everything that you *thought* was so important will pale in comparison to the regret in your heart caused by the knowledge that you cheated your child and yourself out of the special opportunities that come only once in a lifetime. It really comes down to what is important to you.

A story is told about a dad who was a busy man but he finally consented to take his little boy fishing. The little boy was so excited he got everything ready the night before. He even slept in his fishing clothes, boots and all. He did not want to miss the fishing trip with his dad.

Saturday morning came and true to his word, the dad took the boy fishing . . . well, sort of. He took the boy a few miles down the road to a pond with a huge sign that said: *Starving Trout Farm*. The pond was stocked with fish. Catching them was hardly a challenge, even to a small boy. In just a few minutes, the boy caught his legal limit of fish.

"Dad, let's clean the fish before we take them home and eat them," the excited little boy exclaimed.

"No, let's just pay that man over there to do it," the dad replied.

When the boy and his dad got home, the little boy could hardly wait to show his mom the fish they had caught. The dad walked by and didn't say a word. He went straight to the shower, cleaned up, got dressed, walked back past the child and the mom and, still without saying a word, got in the car and drove off to do what he wanted to do with this day.

The little boy looked at his watch. From the time they had left home to go fishing to the time the dad left to do whatever he felt was more important was a total of fifty-five minutes.

The boy later said, "The best day of my life turned instantly into the worst day of my life. It was the most important day to me because I had looked forward for so long to my dad spending some time with me by going fishing with me. It was the worst day of my life because it verified to me just how insignificant I really was to my father." The man who was supposed to be his boy's hero was too busy.

It's all a matter of perspective, isn't it? What may seem insignificant to you may make a life-changing impression upon your child. A famous nineteenth-century poet kept a diary as a youth. His dad also kept a journal. When the boy was about ten years of age, he and his father went fishing together. Years later, long after both the father and son were dead, someone found both the boy's diary and the father's journal describing the events of that day.

In the son's diary, it read, "Father took me fishing today. It was one of the greatest days of my life. Father taught me many things."

The father's journal for that same day read, "Went fishing with my son today. Did not accomplish much."

If you are too busy today to spend time with your child, when will you ever be less busy? Will you ever really be able to find time for your child? If you are so preoccupied with other things that you are doing a poor job of parenting, what will it take to shake you out of your selfishness? If you are waiting for some quality time to "appear," I have bad news for you. Quality time never "appears." The only time you have is right now. What are you going to do with it?

The Winner's Focus

1. If your children spell love T-I-M-E, how do you spell it?
2. What are your thoughts concerning quality time versus quantity of time? You do not necessarily have to agree with me.
3. In what ways have you been substituting material things for spending time with your child?
4. If you were told that you had only a month to live, what would be your deepest regrets in regard to your children? Okay, assuming you are going to live, what can you do differently that might alleviate those regrets?
5. How much time do you really spend with your child each week? If you want a shock, take a stopwatch and time your conversations, play times, and meals together with your child for a week. You may be quite surprised at the difference between how much time you think you

spend with your child and how much time you actually do spend with your child.

6. What are some changes you can make that will help you to "seize the day" with your child?

7. Write down on a piece of paper what you regard as the absolute best time you have ever had together with your child. Now, without letting your child know what you have written, ask your child what the best time was that you ever spent together. How do the two answers compare?

8. On a scale of one to ten (ten = excellent, one = poor), how are you doing in your attempts to balance your relationship with your spouse and your relationship with your children? What would it take to improve that number?

9. What volunteer or community service groups would you and your child enjoy helping together?

10. The last time your boy or girl asked you to play, were you too busy?

11. Would you punish your children if they intentionally hid the television remote control so you would pay some attention to them?

12

Take Me Out
to the Ball Game

W HAT'S A PARENT to do? Your child wants to participate
in competitive sports, but you are not sure the investment of time, energy, and money is worth it. Whether to allow
a child to compete in organized sports while in elementary
school, middle school, or high school is a major issue for many
parents. It is often a point of conflict between parent and child
and frequently causes friction between the two parents.

I raise this topic because I believe sports can be incredibly
educational and help bring out the winner in your children.
They begin to focus, work hard, and be team players, and those
are just three of the key qualities that make a winner in life.

Partly because of my size and partly because a large number of people know a little bit about my background as an

athlete, I am often asked to comment on the values and dangers of modern competitive sports. Sometimes I surprise people with my response. I say, "If the motives for playing the sport are good, and the coaches are good, and the equipment is good, and if the parents and the children know it is just a game, then fine. Go for it. But if a sport takes on a life of its own, and everything and everyone in your family must accommodate the sport, it becomes a drag on the life of the family. If everyone is happy for a week when you win, and devastated for a week when you lose, the sport has lost its value as a character-builder in your family. It is no longer just a game, and I recommend that you seriously evaluate whether it is worth it for your child to be involved in that sport."

As you may have already guessed, I am more than a little prejudiced on this subject. Sports are a major part of what we do with our children at Big Oak Ranch. While we do not force any child to participate, most of our children want to be involved in competitive sports, not for the sense of competition, but because for the first time in their lives, they have someone cheering them on to victory. Many of our Ranch children have literally never heard anyone yell encouragement for them before coming to Big Oak Ranch.

One of our housedads was on the sidelines one Saturday morning, watching a soccer game in which one of his boys was participating. "Atta boy, Billy!" the dad called when his son made a good play. "Way to go, Billy," he cheered when Billy blocked a shot by the opposing team. Billy was having a great game!

If competitive sports served no other purpose, they would be worth it if they simply helped you to find a reason to cheer on and encourage your children to be winners. Whether your children win the game is not the issue. The issue is whether they give it their best effort, whether they win at life. Competitive sports can help your child develop other values too.

THE BENEFITS OF COMPETITIVE
SPORTS TO YOUR CHILD

Gene Stallings, the former football coach at the University of Alabama, has four daughters and a son. Coach Stallings told me that he would never allow a young man to marry one of his daughters until the young man had met two conditions. First, the young man had to work for Stallings on his ranch in Texas during one of those notoriously hot Texas summers. Stallings wanted to see if the young man was a hard worker who would do his best to provide for Coach Stallings's daughter.

Second, the young man had to have played in some sort of sport. "By participating in competitive sports," Coach Stallings explained, "a person learns discipline, teamwork, focusing on an objective, being a competitor, and having a competitor's fire. You cannot learn that any better, anywhere else, other than in the arena of competition. And that's the kind of man I would like for each of my daughters. I want their husbands to be men who have paid the price that one must pay to compete, because then I will know that they will pay the price to take care of my daughters."

Coach Stallings went on to tell me that he wants his sons-in-law to "know what it feels like to be playing basketball when you think your lungs are going to explode. You keep going because you are down to the last sixty seconds, and you are striving to win the game. Or when you are playing football, when your ribs are hurt, and you have a bad bruise on your leg, you ignore the pain and keep going because you must give it your best shot to win. They must know what it is like to do their part to help win the big game. They should be able to think clearly in the middle of stress and be able to stay focused on their objective. Sports teaches them how not to get rattled when they have to adjust their game plan to meet the objective of winning the game. And they learn to deal with the disappointment and frustration of losing. Only competitive sports can give you that sort of experience, without jeopardizing your life."

I believe there are at least five benefits of competitive sports: learning the will to win, teamwork, dedication and commitment, to focus on a goal, and to deal with the impostors of success and failure. Let me explain.

Will to Win

As I mentioned earlier, my friend Johnny Musso was a great All-America running back for the University of Alabama. He finished third in the Heisman Trophy voting his senior year. I recall one time near the end of a game when Johnny was leaning over in our huddle and could barely stand up. His mouth was bleeding, his fingers were mangled, and his ribs were bruised. The pain was so intense he could not keep the tears from trickling down his face. Our quarterback said, "Johnny, get out of here. You're hurt."

Johnny gritted his teeth and said through the pain, "Don't you tell Coach Bryant I'm hurt. Just call the play."

The offensive coordinator, who did not know about John's condition, called the play down from the press box. It was Option Left: Musso through the left side of the line. Reluctantly, the quarterback called Johnny's play. Johnny Musso, ignoring his pain, took the handoff from the quarterback, twisted and turned through the defense, and scored the winning touchdown. He is one of the fiercest competitors I know; one who would never give up. Not many athletes will be tested as Johnny Musso was, but few things in life can give your child the sort of experience an athlete has in competitive sports, as he reaches down inside and gives more than could be expected in his effort to win.

Teamwork

Besides teaching your child how to suppress his own desires for the good of the team, competitive sports can help your child develop an appreciation for others involved in a team effort and the value of those people who do not always share the limelight but are nonetheless essential to the smooth operation of the team.

One night as I was watching a football game on television, the cameras panned down the sidelines near the end of the game. I was intrigued by the condition of the uniforms and helmets of the various players. The camera focused on an offensive lineman. His uniform was filthy, and his jersey torn and spotted with blood. His helmet was scratched and marked with paint the color of the opposing team's helmets, and the protective coating on the face mask was torn off. Although this player had obviously been in the thick of the battle, I could not recall hearing his name since the beginning of the telecast. He had received little if any notice, yet he had obviously done his job effectively.

The camera moved from the lineman to the field-goal kicker. The kicker's uniform was practically spotless. His helmet was smooth and clean. Yet the kicker had put the ball through the uprights three times that night to win the game for his team.

Both of the men were on the team. One got down and dirty and nobody noticed, the other player was slick, shiny, and precise, and millions of people recognized his achievement. Both of the players were essential to the winning effort. It's called teamwork, and apart from the military, few things in life teach it to your child better than competitive sports.

Dedication and Commitment

My daughter is playing basketball for the University of Alabama now. If she wants to make the starting five she is going to have to work harder than the other girls who want to play too. I told her, "Reagan, if you want to play college basketball, you have to be committed. That means when everyone else is going down to the river to go boating, you may have to go to the gym to shoot baskets for an extra hour. When everyone else quits running after doing twenty wind sprints, you may have to run twenty-five sprints to be better prepared than the next person."

Certainly, your child can learn dedication and commitment in all sorts of areas. But dedication and commitment are absolutely necessary in the heat of intense competition, and a sport is a great, fun way to help your child experience them.

To Focus on a Goal

During Reagan's high school basketball career, she blew out the anterior cruciate ligament deep within her knee. She had to have a complete reconstruction. Reagan has always been a natural athlete and has had God-given quickness and agility. Conditioning was a breeze for her. After the surgery, for the first time in Reagan's high school athletic career, she had to really work. She had to exercise the knee and the muscles every day, lift weights, and learn to run all over again. Beyond the physical work, Reagan had to work through her insecurity in using her repaired knee. She knew that the only way to get well was to work, work, work. There were no shortcuts. She did it—she came back stronger and in better shape than ever. She learned what it means to focus on the goal and to keep going until you get there. That is a great benefit competitive sports and the preparation involved with them might help develop in your child.

To Deal with the Impostors of Success and Failure

Both success and failure are impostors because they promise more than they deliver: Winning promises more lasting satisfaction than it truly provides, and losing is never as devastating as it seems at the time. Success in athletics often causes your child to have an inflated opinion of himself; failure in competitive sports can make your child feel that he is worthless. Both of these are lies. But your child may never learn how to deal with the joy of winning and the frustration of losing any easier than on the training ground of competitive sports.

NOBODY CAN OUTWORK YOU

Don Shula, the former coach of the Miami Dolphins, is one of the most successful coaches in the history of professional football. In 1972, before every game, while the other team was coming out onto the field, Coach Shula told his players waiting in the opposite tunnel to come out onto the field something like this: "Men, they might be better prepared than we are. They might have a better game plan. They might even have better athletes than we do. But we are the ones who determine whether they will outwork us or not. Let's set our minds to outwork our opponents and make up for any deficiencies we might have. Remember, nobody can outwork us. Now, let's go do our jobs."

Coach Shula's approach worked. The Miami Dolphins went 17–0 that year and won the Super Bowl, posting the only perfect season to date in modern NFL history. Don Shula's method of motivating his men is a great example for parents to emulate with their children. Parents can prepare their children for life as best they can. They teach them, help them focus, and they point them in the direction of the goal. After that, the remainder is up to the children themselves.

Competitive sports can help you as the parent to encourage your children to work hard to be their best. But they can pose several potential dangers to your children, and you should definitely be aware of them.

THE DANGERS OF COMPETITIVE SPORTS

Injury

One of the most dangerous things about competitive sports is the possibility of injury. Parents should consider carefully the possibility of their children getting hurt before allowing them to play. In football, basketball, baseball, track and field, hockey, soccer, ballet, ice skating, tennis, or gymnastics, injuries occur. Even golfers sometimes get hurt. Your child might fall and break a bone. He might damage his knees or take a blow to the head. Obviously, the odds of getting hurt rise if your child is involved in contact sports such as football or hockey, but even in noncontact sports, you cannot totally protect your child from injury. And you should not try to do so. He cannot spend his whole life tiptoeing on eggshells because he is afraid of getting hurt. In fact, most of the truly great players I have known override their fears in their quest for the goal. It is not that they are unaware of the possibility of injury. They have decided that the goal is worth the risk, and they move forward with gritty determination.

During my college career and afterward, I endured thirteen operations on my knees. While I was in the hospital for the final surgery—when both knees were being operated on in the same procedure—a nurse asked me, "Was it worth it?"

Without hesitation, I answered, "Yes, it was. I'd do it again if I could."

On the other hand, it might surprise you to learn that Tee and I would not allow Brodie to play Pee Wee football. Brodie was distraught; he wanted to play. "How come, Dad? Why can't I play? A lot of the other kids my age are going to play. Why can't I?"

I placed my hands around Brodie's neck to measure it. Then I removed my hands and showed Brodie the circumference I had made with my fingers. "See this, Bro?" I said. "Your whole life is wrapped up in the nerves going to the stem of your brain through this circle less than fourteen inches in circumference. Your body is not ready for the collisions you might have playing Pee Wee football."

"But, Dad," Brodie protested. "Tom is playing." Tom was one of Brodie's friends whose body was slightly larger and more mature.

"That may be so," I replied. "But you are not. When you are a little bigger, then we will discuss it again, but for now your mom and I have made our decision."

Pat Dye, former football coach at Auburn University, once told me that in his opinion the ninth grade was early enough to put a boy into competitive contact football. "Let your child play other games, " Pat said. "Let him play soccer. It has a lot of the same action as football, but it does not have the constant violent contact."

Obsession with Winning

A second danger of competitive sports for your child is that he or she will develop an obsession with winning. Certainly, much of this will depend on your attitude toward your child's participation, but even without your prodding, winning can become addictive.

Please understand, I believe in playing to win. The entire purpose of this book is to help you bring out the winner in your child. But there is more to winning at life than merely winning the big game, or becoming a cheerleader, or getting the top grades. If we are not careful, it is easy to give the impression that winning is all that matters. When that happens, an obsession with the sport can easily overcome your child.

In some schools, for example, if a guy doesn't play football and date a cheerleader, he is worthless. That creates a problem for about 98 percent of the student body. After all, there are only so many positions on a football team, and there are only so many cheerleaders! How silly to base your child's self-worth, and your own, on whether he or she succeeds as an athlete. Be careful! This can happen unintentionally.

The wise parent teaches his child that it is okay to be a gifted athlete, but it is equally fine to be a less-than-great athlete. It is wonderful to be a straight-A student, but if the best your child can do is to make B's, you need to accept that too. (Always remember, though, it is amazing what a little encouragement can do.)

Living Your Dreams Through Your Child

A third danger to your child as a result of competitive sports usually goes hand in hand with the second. The sport can become an obsession in the child's life. This danger may be even more damaging than an obsession with winning. A fine line exists between cheering your child on to victory and living out your own dreams *through* your child. I can't really tell you where that line will be because it is different for every parent and child, but if your child is involved in competitive sports more for you than he is for himself, you have crossed the line.

A few years ago I watched a movie titled *Rudy*, in which the lead character was talking to a fellow player on the Notre Dame football squad. The player sat on the bench with his head in his hands and confessed, "I want to quit, but I can't."

"Why not?" asked Rudy.

"Because my dad was an All-America player here at Notre Dame, so he wants me to play at Notre Dame too. He said he will not pay for me to go to college anywhere else but Notre Dame. So I have to keep getting pounded every day."

It is always sad when a child feels he must participate in sports or anything else merely to feed Mom or Dad's ego. Sometimes it is more than sad; many times it can be downright destructive.

Stephen was a talented athlete, and early in his life, Stephen's dad recognized his potential. Consequently, Stephen's dad committed himself to the job of making his son into a world-class athlete, regardless of the cost. He allowed Stephen to eat only an athlete's diet. Stephen worked out on the best equipment. He went to all the best sports camps. He practiced and trained, with his dad looking over his shoulder all the while. Stephen's dad did not allow his son to participate in many of the normal high school events because, after all, Stephen was in training.

Stephen worked hard, harder than any amateur athlete should be expected to work. He did in fact become a great player. He received the highest honors a high school and college athlete could attain, all-state, All-America, and a high draft selection to the pros.

Once in the professional ranks, however, Stephen was no longer the best player on the team. He was one of many best among the best. And he couldn't handle it. More specifically, his dad could not handle it.

Stephen began to take drugs to compensate for his "failure" and to ease the pain in his heart of letting his dad down. Eventually, he crashed and burned, dropped out of sports altogether, his life in shambles. He said, "I never wanted to be a star athlete in the first place. I was just playing because Dad kept pushing me."

Over the years, I have met hundreds of men and women who were driven to "success" in a certain area by their mothers or fathers when in fact that person had no interest in the field Mom or Dad forced them to pursue. Even as adults, they remain despondent because they cannot live up to their parents' expectations.

If your children are playing for you rather than themselves, you need to reduce the pressure to be involved in the sport. Of course you want to motivate your children, you want to encourage them to be the best they can be; you want your children to learn how to work hard, to sacrifice, and go for the goal. When it comes to amateur sports, though, if your children are not having fun, it may not be worth it. Make sure your children are having fun.

WHAT SPORTS ARE REALLY ABOUT

It is not the children who usually lose sight of the fun sports are supposed to be, it is the parents. I attended a Little League baseball game not long ago in which the umpire made a close call. The father of the boy involved in the play loudly yelled a litany of expletives in the direction of the umpire. As if that wasn't bad enough, the man stormed up to the umpire, made several more derogatory remarks about the umpire's parentage, and then slugged him! All this happened right in front of thirty Little Leaguers to whom we were supposed to be teaching good sportsmanship! That man crossed the line, and if he doesn't get a grip on what the purpose for these games is meant to be, he is going to destroy not only his reputation in the community, he is going to destroy his child.

In this regard, moms are often just as bad as dads. I once noticed a woman who was cheering at her child's game. Actually, I couldn't help noticing the woman. Every time her son got on base, the woman went bonkers! She was yelling and applauding and screaming as though her son had just won the World Series. She was equally demonstrative in a negative way when her son struck out. It was as though the end of the world had come, merely because her boy had missed a baseball. How do you think he felt when he heard his mom screaming at him because he didn't succeed that time at bat? The best baseball players in the world average getting on base only one out of every three times at bat. While I am an advocate of cheering your child on to victory, as parents we need to lighten up and keep the game in perspective.

A few years ago, the nation reeled in horror when it learned of Wanda Holloway's plot to have Verna Heath and her fourteen-year-old daughter, Amber, snuffed out by a paid killer. The motive behind the misguided mother's malicious deeds made her crime even more appalling: Wanda was angry that Amber had been chosen for the junior high cheerleading squad instead of her own daughter, Sharma. The girls, who lived around the block from each other, had attended the same Christian elementary school and had even cheered together on the same squad before going to junior high. Sharma's mom, Wanda, played the organ at church.

We need to keep our children's competitive sports or other extracurricular activities in balance. Moderation is the key. If your child wants to be a cheerleader, let her go to cheerleading camp. What if she does not want to become a cheerleader? Let her find some other activity she enjoys.

I know the positive impact that competitive sports have had in my life, and I am happy that my children enjoy sports as well. But if my children had no interest in participating in sports, that would be okay with Tee and me. Why? Because we love them for who they are, and we want our children to pursue their dreams, not ours.

I once met an eighteen-year-old young woman at a place where I was speaking. The girl was bawling her eyes out. When she finally gained her composure enough to tell me what was troubling her, she said, "My dad always wanted a boy rather than a girl. When I was born and he found out that I was a girl, he left the hospital because he was so bitterly disappointed. Nothing I do is ever good enough for him. Dad has never really loved me, simply because I am not a boy."

How sad! That father missed eighteen years of his daughter's life and did severe damage to her self-image, all because he wanted to live out his unfulfilled dreams through a son he did not have. Sometimes we lose sight of the real trophies in life.

Charles Barkley, the former star basketball player for the Houston Rockets, is a friend of the children at Big Oak Ranch. One night, when he played for the Phoenix Suns, I attended a game in Phoenix in which the Suns soundly whipped the Atlanta Hawks. Afterward, Charles invited me to go downstairs into the locker room.

The place was jammed with hot, sweaty bodies as the players came in from the court and headed for the showers. Some players were holding ice packs to sore limbs. They looked as though they had been at war.

A throng of reporters gathered around Barkley as a member of the National Basketball Association presented him with an eighteen-inch, specially designed trophy. "Congratulations, Charles," he said. "This trophy is in honor of your achievement of scoring fifteen thousand points so far in your NBA career. We are all very proud of you."

Still dressed in his soaking wet uniform, Charles graciously received the trophy and said, "Thank you very much. I really appreciate this."

Then with the television cameras whirring, and a host of network and local reporters thrusting their microphones closer to his face, Charles turned toward his locker as he said, "I'll put this trophy right here, next to the most important trophy I possess."

With that, Charles Barkley reached into his locker and pulled out a picture of his little girl. Holding the photo up for the cameras, Charles said with a smile, "This is the greatest trophy I have! "

Unfortunately, the national sports shows did not choose to report Charles's statement, but the man was right. The trophies on the fireplace mantel are not our greatest treasures. Our children *are* the most precious trophies we have. If competitive sports help you to bring out the winner in your child, then enjoy them, and help your child to enjoy them. But if your child never tosses a ball, runs a race, or is a member of a dance troupe, a debating team, chess club, or anything else, your child is still a trophy worth cherishing.

THE WINNER'S FOCUS

1. What part did competitive sports play in your childhood? Would you now assess your experience as a positive factor or a negative factor in your growing up?
2. What benefits of competitive sports do you see as the most important?
3. If your child is not involved in competitive sports, how are you cheering him on to be a winner? How are you teaching him about teamwork?
4. What are your thoughts concerning competition itself? Do you see that as a plus or a minus in your child's development?
5. What dangers of competitive sports concern you the most in regard to your child?

6. In your opinion, how do the benefits competitive sports may impart to your child compare to the risks posed by the dangers your child might encounter in competitive sports?

7. How can a sports-parent avoid living vicariously through his or her child's involvement with sports?

13

When to Intervene
in Your Child's Affairs

"HERE SHE COMES! Get ready," Jason said to Dirk, as he elbowed him in the ribs. Jason and Dirk leaned back against their junior high school lockers and crossed their arms in front of their chests.

Pretty Monica Jones was coming down the hallway with two of her school girlfriends. As always, Monica was dressed modestly. Because she had physically matured earlier than most of the other girls in the eighth grade, Monica's body was a constant object of attention and the subject of rude, insensitive, junior high jokes. Jason and Dirk were two of the worst offenders.

When Monica and her friends were only a few steps away from Jason and Dirk, Jason whispered, "Let's go!"

Jason and Dirk stepped into the center of the hallway, blocking the girls' passage. They elbowed their way between Monica and her friends, so Monica was momentarily trapped between Jason on one side of her and Dirk on the other. The two boys grabbed Monica, squeezed her breasts, and then bolted down the hall, screaming and laughing at the top of their voices. Monica burst into tears.

This was not an isolated incident. The two boys had been badgering Monica since the students had returned from summer vacation to school several weeks before. Sometimes it was only Dirk who accosted Monica. Sometimes it was Jason who would grab Monica as she was coming out of class. Often, both boys harassed the girl verbally or physically.

Already self-conscious about her blossoming body, Monica broke into tears of embarrassment every time one of the boys touched her or taunted her. She tried to avoid Jason and Dirk, but it was a small school in a small town, so there was no way to escape their presence all day long. Sooner or later, one or both of the boys always found her.

Monica began to have difficulty concentrating in her classes. Emotionally, she was extremely fragile. She often burst into tears at the slightest mention of Jason's and Dirk's names. Frequently, Monica hid in the restroom until the halls cleared. Then she would go into her classes late in her attempt to miss Jason and Dirk. She finally got to the point that she did not want to go to school at all.

Monica was reluctant to tell her mom and dad about what was happening at school, so she feigned illnesses to stay at home as often as possible. Eventually, however, her parents made her go back to classes. Rather than endure the abuse from Jason and Dirk, Monica began to skip school. She left home each morning, dressed for school, carrying a backpack and books, but she spent most of her days roaming the mall until classes were dismissed. Had the truant officer not called Monica's mom about her attendance record, her parents may not have discovered what was happening to their daughter until some deeper harm came to her.

Monica's parents, both sincere, upright, model citizens, immediately confronted their daughter about her absenteeism. Only then did Monica break down crying and tell her mom and dad about what Jason and Dirk were doing to her at school.

Monica's parents were furious! Her dad wanted to go find the two boys that same night and beat the daylights out of them. Fortunately, Monica's mom, although severely distraught, remained cool enough to realize that her husband's plan would only worsen things. After a while, she was able to calm him down, and the two sat down at the kitchen table to decide what to do. They felt that it was appropriate to call the school principal about the matter.

Still fuming, Monica's dad called the school administrator. After briefly explaining the situation, the dad said, "I want to meet you and those boys and their dads or moms in your office tomorrow."

The principal agreed to arrange a meeting for the following day after school. In the meantime, Monica's dad began making some phone calls to the parents of Monica's friends. Several of them confirmed that their daughters had mentioned something about what the boys had been doing to Monica. The parents agreed to allow their daughters to speak to the principal the following day.

The next afternoon, Monica's father and mother were at the school to face the boys who had been harassing their daughter. Jason's father and Dirk's mother were there as well. Almost immediately after the principal informed the parents of the reason for the meeting and gave a brief account of the situation, Jason's father began defending his boy's crude actions and comments. When his logic began to sound totally ludicrous, he resorted to making accusations against Monica. "Well, your daughter is no angel either," Jason's dad shouted.

"What are you talking about?" Monica's dad demanded.

"Well, she said some ugly things to my boy."

"Like what?" Monica's dad pressed.

"Well, like, the other day, your daughter told my boy to shut up. So he grabbed her."

"By her breast?" the principal wanted to know.

"Well, I don't know where he grabbed her, but that is not the point. . . ."

"No, that is exactly the point," Monica's dad said evenly but firmly. "What your boy did to my daughter was wrong. And I demand an apology. I am here to tell you that it better not ever happen again, or we will not be meeting in a school office. I will press charges against you and your boy, and we will meet in a court of law."

Dirk's mother was embarrassed and disgusted that her son would do such things to Monica. The mother apologized and promised to discipline her son.

Monica's mom and dad were much cooler about handling the situation than you or I might have been in similar circumstances, but the family's story raises a serious issue for parents nowadays: When should you ignore inequities against your child and when should you intervene? Often it is a judgment call. Regrettably, discernment such as this comes only through practice.

When you intervene in your child's affairs too quickly, too frequently, or too extensively, you run the risk of robbing your child of her self-worth. Your child gets the inner picture of a physical, mental, or emotional weakling who cannot do anything for herself. If you continually fight her battles for her, your child will become a paternalistic, psychological cripple. Beyond that, your child will be less likely to tell you things for fear you will overreact and embarrass her even more than the situation itself does.

On the other hand, if you fail to intervene when you should, your child will get the impression that you do not care, that she does not matter, or that the events or circumstances of her life are not important to you. Frequently, such children become distant, reclusive types, who keep their emotions tightly pent up inside, because they feel their parents do not want to deal with their hurts and pains, anyhow. Often such children have difficulty expressing or receiving love and affection.

If the child is strong-willed, she may compensate for her feelings by becoming a gung-ho, self-sufficient, I-don't-need-anyone type of person. Such individuals often have great difficulty in maintaining meaningful, lasting relationships.

Considered from that perspective, knowing when and how to intervene in your child's life takes on a greater significance. Certainly, you should never tolerate physical, mental, or emotional abuse of your child by anyone. If you even suspect such activity, you should intervene immediately, yet carefully. Nor should you allow verbal abuse of your child in the form of degrading talk about his or her character or mental abilities. When comments consistently go beyond the usual sarcasm and verbal cutting up expected between peers, you should consider stepping into the situation. You should also intervene when your child is being put into compromising positions over which she has little or no control.

For instance, Susie was an outstanding member of the high school choral group. Her music director, a male, always insisted that Susie ride alone with him in his car on the way to their performances. The remainder of the choral members rode in the school van. Although nothing improper ever occurred, Susie's dad did not like the appearance that his daughter was being given preferential treatment, or the possibility that his daughter's reputation and moral integrity might be impaired or her safety and well-being jeopardized. The dad intervened and put a stop to the director's practice of having Susie ride with him.

Before You Intervene

When situations arise that you feel merit your getting directly involved with your child's affairs, before you get all steamed up and say or do something foolish or make comments you may later regret, be sure your child is giving you all the accurate information you need to make a wise decision. Certainly, if your child does not have a history of lying, your first inclination will be to believe what your child tells you. That is right and good. Maybe your child is not lying to you, but his perception of the facts is distorted or is merely a matter of opinion. Is the teacher at school really picking on your child because he hassles him about having his homework in on time? Or is that a matter of your child's perception of the facts?

You may need to do some investigative work on your own, as Monica's dad did by calling the parents of Monica's friends. Whatever it takes, be sure to take the time to get the facts before you confront. You may save your child and yourself a great deal of grief later on by getting the facts straight first.

When we first began Big Oak Ranch, a local woman called to complain that one of those "Ranch boys" had spoken to her teenage daughter in rude terms. We set up a meeting for that night at my house on the Ranch property. Before the meeting, I talked to the accused boy, and he gave me a completely different perspective on the facts.

We met that night and immediately the mom set off on a ten-minute tirade about how "sorry" and "no account" the boy was. I sat quietly until the woman was finished with her outburst. Then I showed her more than a dozen letters in her daughter's own handwriting that her daughter had sent to the boy. In the letters, the girl shared explicit details of what she wanted to do with and have done to her by the boy. The mom read the letters and was embarrassed and angry. She stormed out of the house and never said another word to me about the matter. She had made the mistake of not getting her facts straight before confronting.

The boy told me later that night that the girl had been attempting to seduce him for several weeks before she started writing the notes. The boy had been too embarrassed to say anything to anyone. Before he went to bed that night, he stopped and said to me, "Thanks. No one has ever stood up for me before."

Along the same line, keep in mind there are always two sides to a story when your child has a conflict with someone else, and your tendency as a parent will be to side with your child. For this reason, it is often helpful to seek the advice of a pastor, counselor, or trusted friend before you intervene. For instance, a schoolteacher accused Christie of taking ten dollars out of the teacher's purse. The teacher had not seen Christie steal the money, but another child accused Christie.

When the school principal called Christie's parents about the matter, they were convinced that the snitch was the real culprit. "She is just jealous of our daughter, so she is trying to get Christie in trouble," Christie's mom told the principal. The principal held his ground but said he would look further into the matter.

In the meantime, Christie's mom called a friend for some advice on how to handle the situation. The friend attended the same church as Christie's family. When she realized the reason Christie's mom was calling, the friend said, "Well, I guess now would be a good time to tell you that last summer at church camp, I saw your daughter take five dollars out of another girl's purse. I didn't want to say anything, because I did not want to stir up trouble. It was only five dollars, and I conveniently dropped another five-dollar bill near the girl from whom the money was stolen so she would find it and not be out the money. I thought it was just a one-time thing with Christie, but maybe I was wrong."

"Are you sure about this?" asked Christie's mom.

"I saw it with my own eyes," her friend assured her.

When Christie's mom confronted her daughter about the money stolen at the church camp, Christie was flabbergasted. To Christie, it was as though the voice of God was speaking to her. After all, her mom had not been at the church camp. How could she possibly know about the stolen five dollars? Christie burst into tears and confessed stealing both the five dollars at church camp and the ten dollars out of the teacher's purse.

Had Christie's mother not taken the time to seek an outside perspective, she may have insistently stood up for her daughter. When she discovered the truth, she admitted the matter to the school principal and agreed to the principal's suggested discipline of Christie. Christie's mom and dad had some discipline of their own to apply to Christie as well.

WHEN YOU DISAGREE WITH YOUR CHILD'S SCHOOL

Once upon a time in America, it could be assumed that the public school system and the family were complementary to each other. That cannot always be said nowadays. Many parents are finding that some of their children's public school curriculums are more likely to undermine the role of the parents than to support it. Consequently, more parents are scrutinizing what their children are being taught. From New York, where a parent-led protest of a school district's effort to include homosexually oriented materials in the curriculum resulted in the offensive materials being removed, to Texas, where parents have fought for the rights of their children to have voluntary Bible clubs on school property, parents are realizing that they cannot sit back idly and depend upon the school to reinforce the values parents are teaching at home. Concerning the trends in public education, one person commented wryly, "Little Johnny can put a condom on a zucchini, but he can't read. Little Johnny is a global citizen but he can't do basic math. Little Johnny can't write a full paragraph without making a mistake, but he is politically correct."

What can you do as a parent to safeguard your child's education? First and foremost, know your child well enough to recognize when things are going well and when they are not. In this regard, it is imperative that you move beyond superficial communication about your child's school experiences.

Imagine that when your child comes home from school, you ask, "How was school today, honey?"

Your child responds, "Fine."

If you allow the conversation to end there, that is all you will know about your child's day at school. You will not find out about the reprimand your child received from the teacher. You will not hear about the little boy who chased your daughter around the playground, trying to scare her with some earthworms. Nor will you hear about the teacher's encouraging words to your child when she turned in the best report in the class. If you want to be ready to intervene when necessary, you must enter into your child's life at school when the two of you are at home.

Second, know what is being taught in your school system. Two plus two will always equal four (I hope!), but more and more, other subjects are open to a wide variety of interpretations.

For example, what slant on American history is your child being taught? What textbooks are being used? What materials are being read in literature classes? What art is being studied and at what level? All of these are questions you will not know answers to unless you take time to become familiar with your child's school materials. If you are not sure what is being taught in a course, ask to see a syllabus or a teacher's daily plan book.

Third, get to know your child's schoolteachers. Do not be reluctant to schedule conferences with your child's teachers, and do not hesitate to question the teachers about your child's progress academically, socially, and emotionally.

Fourth, if possible, become involved in your local parent-teacher organization or similar auxiliary group that supports your child's school. These groups will help you stay abreast of what is happening at your child's school and also alert you to problems. Moreover, your school board will usually entertain suggestions from the PTO much quicker than those from individual parents. Make your voice heard.

Fifth, seek the input of other parents. Often your child's friends might tell their parents about potential problem areas concerning your child even before the teachers are aware the problems exist. In Monica's case, for example, the children had mentioned to their parents the way Jason and Dirk were treating Monica. Besides, parents need all the support and encouragement they can get. The parents of your child's classmates are going through many of the same joys and frustrations that you are. Parents of your child's classmates may prove to be an invaluable pool of helpful information and camaraderie.

Do not be afraid to stand up for what is right when something in your child's school program violates your values. If the content of a course offends you, let the proper authorities know about it. Do not sit back and wait for someone else to speak up if the school attempts to take over the role of the church or the family in your child's life. You must speak and you must act, yet do so in a helpful and informed manner. Don't go off half-cocked!

Some folks might agree with you and others may disagree. That is not the issue. The issue is simply pursuing what is best for your child and what will best help bring out the winner in him or her.

Finally, you must intervene when the school or someone representing the school (or anyone else) insults your child's honor with a lewd remark or attacks him personally by cursing or the like. During my senior year of high school, my basketball coach verbally assaulted me in the middle of the basketball court in front of five thousand people in the fieldhouse. It was one of the last games of the season, so I had little recourse other than to absorb the public humiliation and go on. I played the entire second half of the game seething. I rebounded, scored points, and played hard, but I didn't care about that. I was furious with that coach. What little respect I had for him prior to that game was gone.

My dad was in the stands that Friday night when the coach ripped into me. On Monday morning, my dad was in the school office waiting to talk to the principal. The principal had no trouble guessing what Dad wanted to talk about. Dad told the principal, "I want to talk with the basketball coach."

The principal stonewalled, "Well, Mr. Croyle, I don't think—" Dad waved him off. "I will talk to the coach here, or I will wait and talk to him after school, but it would be better if I talked to him here," Dad said forcefully. "We need to address this right now."

"Er, ah, well . . . yes. I understand, Mr. Croyle." The principal called for the basketball coach, and he and my dad began to talk.

My dad made it clear that he would not tolerate another public tirade toward me by that coach.

"Well, I might have made a mistake," said the coach.

"It seems to me that after having been an assistant coach last year and having my son play for you all this year as well that you would know by now that yelling and screaming at him in front of five thousand people is not the way to get him to do his best."

"I may not have handled it very well," the coach conceded.

"It had better never happen again," my dad warned.

Interestingly, this was the first time in eighteen years of my life that I can recall my dad ever confronting someone to defend me. Dad would not intervene in my childhood conflicts, but this was different. Dad knew the coach had done more than reprimand me as a player. The coach had attacked me as a person; he had attacked my good name, my character, my reputation, my integrity. And to my dad, that was a time to intervene on the behalf of his eighteen-year-old son.

Never be complacent about what's going on in your child's life. You do not want to be a pest about intervening on the part of your child; all of us have seen overly sensitive parents who are in the principal's office nearly every day complaining about some minor issue. But there are times when you need to stick up for your child, and don't be bashful about it. Discernment and balance are the keys.

SPOTTING THE SIGNS OF
DRUG ABUSE IN YOUR CHILD

Our children are exposed to so many negative aspects of life nowadays, due to our global communications networks and the immediacy of television news coverage. In the past, children may have heard of sexual abuse, alcoholism, or drug addiction, but many children had never encountered victims of such compulsive behavior. Many of us who are parents today never met a bona fide drug user until we were in our late teens or early college years. Although we now know that some of our childhood friends were being abused by their parents, most of us were totally unaware of such perversions during our childhood.

Times have changed. Even if your children do not personally know someone who is in trouble because of drugs, sex, alcohol, eating disorders, or child abuse—which is probably rare—they are much more aware that these things are happening all around them. Ironically, despite better educational efforts and greater access to information, children still are getting hooked on alcohol, nicotine, and drugs; children are still being seduced or coerced into abusive situations. More than ever as a parent, you need to be vigilant in learning how to spot the warning signs that something major may be going wrong in the life of your child.

Some doctors can look at a patient and, before doing an in-depth examination, see the symptoms of certain problems. Similarly, after working with children for more than twenty years, I have come to be able to spot signs that might indicate that something is out of whack in the life of a child.

When a child is brought in to my office to meet me, the first thing I notice is the eyes of the child. Many times the eyes will give me a clue of what is going on in his life. Some children have "soft" eyes. They come in and are as nervous and apprehensive as little fawns. Others are so trusting, so naive. Other children have "strained" eyes; they are filled with anger, resentment, bitterness, frustration, or apprehension. They have had a hard life and their eyes tell the story. Still other children have "shark" eyes. Looking into the eyes of these children is like looking into the eyes of a corpse. They are empty, hollow, expressionless, indifferent to all that is happening around them, just like a shark's.

Get in the habit of looking into your child's eyes when you speak to him. Although you won't always be able to specifically pinpoint what sort of problem your child is having by the look in his eyes, you will hopefully be able to tell when something is wrong.

Changes in attitude or in your child's tone of voice are often signs that something is happening about which you should be concerned. Certainly, as your children mature, especially in their early teens, they will be changing right before your eyes, often much more quickly than you would care to see happen. You need not be concerned over every little transformation as your child moves through adolescence. On the other hand, do not ignore changes in your child's overall countenance, eating habits, personal hygiene, secrecy—especially regarding the use of money or its disappearance around your home. Notice, too, any drastic changes in your child's preference of friends. Pay attention if your child receives phone calls from friends who refuse to give you their names, or if you are receiving an unusually high number of telephone calls in which the caller hangs up when you or some other adult answers the phone.

Many parents can tell when something is going haywire in their child's life. Obviously, you must intervene if your child comes home intoxicated or reeks of marijuana. Swift, consistent discipline may save your child from going down a slippery slope of alcohol or drug abuse.

Drug abuse is tougher for many parents to spot, especially if they have never had any involvement with drugs themselves. In his outstanding book, *Dare to Discipline*, Dr. James Dobson lists eight physical and emotional symptoms that may indicate substance abuse by your child.

1. Inflammation of the eyelids and nose is common. The pupils of the eyes are either very wide or very small, depending on the kind of drugs internalized.
2. Extremes of energy may be represented. Either the individual is sluggish, gloomy, and withdrawn, or he may be loud, hysterical, and jumpy.
3. The appetite is extreme—either very great or very poor. Weight loss may occur.
4. The personality suddenly changes; the individual may become irritable, inattentive, and confused, or aggressive, suspicious, and explosive.
5. Body and breath odor is often bad. Cleanliness is generally ignored.
6. The digestive system may be upset—diarrhea, nausea, and vomiting may occur. Headaches and double vision are also common. Other signs of physical deterioration may include change in skin tone and body stance.
7. Needle marks on the body, usually appearing on the arms, are an important symptom. These punctures sometimes get infected and appear as sores and boils.
8. Moral values often crumble and are replaced by new, way-out ideas and values.[1]

Don't see symptoms of a disease that are not there. But if you notice one or more of these indicators, do not ignore them. Act upon them. Do not think, *If I give him time, my child will eventually come to his senses.* Wrong! You are already behind in this battle by the time you discover that the compulsive behaviors have begun, but it is never too late to fight. Whatever triggered the behavior may have ceased, but that does not mean the behavior itself will stop without drastic action being taken.

Never underestimate the addictive power of compulsive behavior. Your child will not come to his senses without help. Granted, if your child is to get out of trouble, it will require a desire to do so on his part. But you must help. You must intervene in your child's life.

RECOGNIZING SIGNS OF
SEXUAL ABUSE IN YOUR CHILD

Nearly every week someone asks me, "Is sexual abuse more rampant nowadays?" I do not think so; the issue is simply more publicized than it has been in the past. Ironically, with more information about sexual abuse available, and more victims going public about abuse in their pasts, we run the risk of becoming jaded and calloused by the constant barrage of horror stories coming to light. But we dare not get used to the issue of sexual abuse. It is a problem many of our children face every day.

For many parents, sexual abuse may be such an awkward subject, or is such an emotionally charged issue, that it is difficult to discuss it. Nevertheless, if your child is being abused, you cannot ignore it! David Peters, in his book *Betrayal of Innocence*, shares a few signs to look for that might indicate that your child is being or has been sexually abused:

1. Being uncomfortable around previously trusted persons
2. Sexualized behavior (excessive masturbation, sexually inserting objects, explicit sex play with other children, etc.)
3. Fear of restrooms, showers, or baths (common locations of abuse)
4. Fear of being alone with men or boys
5. Nightmares on a regular basis or about the same person
6. Abrupt personality changes

7. Uncharacteristic hyperactivity
8. Moodiness, excessive crying
9. Aggressive or violent behavior toward other children
10. Difficulty in sleeping or relaxing
11. Clinging behavior that may take the form of separation anxiety
12. Passive or withdrawn behavior[2]

In most cases of sexual abuse, the perpetrator is known by the victim. Whether the offender is a friend or a member of the family, whether distant or close, the issue must be dealt with.

You may not want to deal with it. But it will do you no good to live in denial. Denying to yourself and to others that something wrong is going on in the life of your child can do irreparable damage to your child and to your relationship with him. This is a delicate issue, but you must realize that this situation exists and respond to it correctly to help repair your child's life. Stories abound of adults who were abused as children, but nobody believed them or tried to help them. They are now scarred for life.

If your child is being abused by somebody else and you need help in dealing with the situation, contact a local counseling center for assistance. If you are the offending abuser, you must seek help for yourself immediately. Don't hesitate.

THE WINNER'S FOCUS

1. Describe a time when your parents did not intervene on your behalf. Looking back, do you now regard their lack of intervention as an opportunity for you to learn a valuable lesson, or do you regard it as a failure on your parents' part to understand the circumstances you were facing? Why?

2. When your parents did intervene on your behalf, how did you respond? Were you embarrassed? Grateful? Indifferent? As an adult, if something similar happened to your child, what would you do differently?

3. Have you ever intervened in your child's circumstances without having all the facts and were made to look like a fool? How did you respond?

4. Has your child ever had a close adult friend, and you noticed your child do a 180-degree turn in her attitude toward that person?

5. Have there been times you suspected improper affections on the part of an older person toward your child? What did you do? Did you ask your child about the situation? Did you confront the older person involved? Remember, respond, do not react.

6. Do you look your child in the eyes when you talk to him? Does your child look you in the eyes when he speaks to you?

7. As a parent, how can you learn a balance concerning standards of intervention in your child's life?

14

Keeping on Course

I HAVE BEEN AROUND ranch life for more than two decades. Over the years, I have noticed a lot of interesting parallels between the ways some of our ranch animals behave and the various ways children sometimes act. Let me explain.

Some of our four-legged creatures at Big Oak Ranch are not horses; they are mules. Even the best of mules is still stubborn, stupid, and is intent on doing things his way and no other. A mule sees only one course: one he wants to run.

Through the years some of our horses have been Shetland ponies. A little Shetland pony is cocky, arrogant, prances around a lot, and is all for show. The Shetland, although he is often quite cute, has one major problem. He confuses activity with accomplishment. Have you ever seen a Shetland pony on a race track? He is moving; his little legs and hooves are hustling as fast as he can go, but he doesn't cover much ground.

Shetland ponies are fun to watch, but they don't usually win many races.

Then there is the thoroughbred horse. The thoroughbred is disciplined, well trained, focused; he knows where he is supposed to go, and he is willing to give everything he has to get there. When riding a thoroughbred, all the jockey needs to do is to lightly touch the horse's flank, and the horse responds to the rider's directions by changing course or speed. The horse has been disciplined to stay within his boundaries and to run the race for the prize.

I once asked an owner of championship racehorses how to tell an excellent horseman. Without hesitating, the owner replied, "Watch his hands." The owner went on to explain that if the jockey tugs or pulls at the reins, either he is not a good horseman or the horse has not been well trained. It is similar to the rack-and-pinion steering mechanism on a finely tuned automobile. It takes only a slight movement of the hands on the wheel to drastically alter the course of the auto. Similarly, the horse owner emphasized, a good horseman needs to exert only slight pressure on a thoroughbred horse to bring about a positive course correction. I couldn't help thinking, *The same thing is true with children. The better trained the child, as the child gets older, the less pressure the parent needs to apply to bring about a positive course correction, because the training has accomplished the desired purpose—to produce a winner.*

Interestingly, I have noticed that well-trained thoroughbreds prefer to run with thoroughbreds; mules stick with the other mules, and Shetlands love to waste away their days prancing around with other Shetlands. It is hilarious to see a mule trying to be a thoroughbred. It is heartbreaking to see a thoroughbred lose sight of what he was made to be and start acting like a mule or a Shetland pony.

Moreover, I have never seen a mule produce a thorough-bred racehorse. Occasionally, I have seen thoroughbred horses that were not adequately disciplined or were allowed to lose sight of the prize set before them.

As parents, we want our children to be champions. If that is your desire, remember this: You reproduce what you are. If you are a stubborn mule or a prancing Shetland, the chances of your producing a winner are negligible. On the other hand, if you are a thoroughbred—even if you weren't born that way—you can impart those characteristics to your child. With our children, being a thoroughbred has more to do with the quality of the training received than it does with genetics. And the quality of the training usually closely parallels the time invested by the parent in the training process.

Some parents work hard to give their children all sorts of material things, but they forget to teach their children values that are truly important, the courage and character to say no to what is not good for them and to say yes to those things that are. How many children have wiped out because the parents lost their focus on what is important? They took their eyes off the prize. Or somehow they got confused, charted the wrong course for their children, and led them hastily down the wrong path. Sadly, many times parents think they are on the right road when in fact they are not.

YOU NEED AN ACCURATE COMPASS

It is easy to get sidetracked in your efforts to bring out the winner in your child, especially if your course is being set by false or inaccurate information. I once watched a movie in which a man and a woman were flying through a storm at night in a small airplane. The rain, wrapped in a cold, whistling wind, pelted the plane as the pilot attempted to wrestle the small aircraft through the treacherous mountains looming all around them. Inky darkness and thick fog conspired to suck up the beam of the plane's small light, leaving the couple with no alternative but to put the plane on autopilot and to trust their flight—and their lives—to the plane's instruments. The man navigated solely by means of the plane's compass.

Because the man was peering so intently at the instrument panel, he paid no attention when the woman placed a metal container full of coffee near the plane's compass. Minutes ticked by, and the storm raged on unabated.

"We should have been there by now," the man fretted to the woman. "Something must be wrong. Let's check the latitude and longitude again."

The pilot looked at his map and then back toward the compass. It was then that he noticed the metal coffee container sitting near the compass. To his terror, he saw that the magnetic tip of the compass was attracted to the metal! The compass was not pointing toward true north as it was supposed to. That meant that the plane was not flying in the correct direction! They were lost. Worse yet, they were not flying out of the mountains, toward their destination. They were flying right toward the mountains! While they thought they had been charting their course by the magnetic North Pole, the craft had actually been charting its own course. It was an accident just waiting to happen.

The man grabbed the metal container and threw it as far back in the plane, away from the compass, as he could pitch it. In the nick of time, just before the plane crashed into a mountain, he was able to make a course correction and the couple came through the storm safely. They had almost lost it all because of the inaccurate compass.

Many parents have come close to doing something similar. They have been charting their course according to faulty or inadequate information. Your job as a parent is similar to the task of that couple in that cockpit. All sorts of attractive distractions can easily get you off course as you maneuver through this mountainous maze we call parenting. Some of those things may make your compass needle bounce all over the place, and by doing so, they can distort the accuracy of your compass.

You must keep your eye on the compass and make sure that the lens is clean. If the compass by which you are guiding your life—and your child's life—is not clear of potential distortions, you will think that you are going in the right direction when you aren't. If you stubbornly insist upon following its faulty information, you will inevitably choose a deflected course that will lead you to confusion, despair, disorientation—and ultimately to destruction.

Imagine, for instance, that you have your sights focused on your child being rich, or at least richer than you! Your compass needle is pointing toward having the best education, nice cars, the fancy home, belonging to the right clubs, wearing all the right clothes, and being seen in all the right places. What you don't realize is that your compass is giving you undependable readings. Your child will never be truly happy because riches alone cannot bring inner peace. The news is filled almost daily with stories of fabulously wealthy men and women whose lives are in utter turmoil. Is that what you want for your child? Maybe you have been doing a great job at achieving your goal of helping your child attain riches. You have been making great progress; you have been making great time. Unfortunately, you have been charting the course of your life and that of your child by a confused compass.

Maybe you allowed your compass to become distorted long ago. Perhaps you allowed bright, shiny attractions and distractions to somehow get too close to your heart. In the process, the guiding principles upon which you once charted your life became confused and unreliable. If so, it will take courage to admit that you have made a mistake, that you have been charting your course by the wrong compass, or in actuality, that your compass has been charting your course for you according to inaccurate information.

It is not too late to change directions, but it will take an act of will to do so. You must make up your mind that you are willing to change. To bring out the winner in your child, you must first be certain that you are on the right track yourself.

Getting on the Right Path

Imagine you are driving down an interstate highway. You are driving the right vehicle, at the right speed, on the right road. But suddenly you realize that you are going in the wrong direction. What do you do? You could keep going in the wrong direction for the next twelve hours. That might expose you to a lot of fascinating scenery, but you would be no closer to your destination.

Of course, you really have only two choices if you want to end up in the right place. You can make a series of midcourse corrections or you can stop, get off on an exit, turn around, and start going in the right direction. Take enough midcourse corrections, and eventually you might get on the right road; it will take you a lot longer, and you will lose a lot of time. Besides that, you always run the risk of getting lost during your corrective process. On the other hand, the abrupt turn-around may be radical, but it may prove to be the wisest move you could make. If you refuse to turn around, your error may turn into a mistake.

I was in Florida with a group of boys from Big Oak Ranch when several of the boys got in some serious trouble. We were staying in an apartment complex and I met with them in the living room. I was really racking my brain, trying to figure out how I could reach those boys and help them get back on the right track. I prayed, "God, please give me some insight concerning these boys and something I can say or do that will help them."

As I looked over their shoulders I saw a bumper sticker at the top of the clothes rack that read, "An error does not become a mistake until you refuse to correct it."

That's it! I thought. "Boys! Look behind you," I instructed the fellows sitting on the couch. "Read that bumper sticker."

"An error does not become a mistake until you refuse to correct it," one of the boys read aloud.

"That's right. And that is the truth," I told them. "Now you boys have made some serious errors. But we do not need to allow those errors to go on any longer. We can start to correct them beginning today." All but one of these boys did a 180-degree turn in their attitudes and got on the right track. The one boy continued down the wrong road, and we had to resort to firmer actions and disciplines.

Similarly, you and I have made many errors in our lives. Many of our errors directly affect the lives of our children. We need not allow those errors to turn into mistakes. We can begin to make the corrections today.

The first step is to get on the right path. The compass to help you make sure you are moving in the right direction is the Bible. It is the one true compass; you can depend upon it to provide you with accurate information upon which you can base your entire life. The Bible will also give you a wealth of wisdom to help you bring out the winner in your child.

THE PATH AND THE WAY

Once you find the right path, it is important how you walk on it. The Bible says, "Make me know Thy ways, O Lord; / Teach me Thy paths" (Psalm 25:4). The path is where your feet are walking; the way you proceed down the path makes all the difference in the world.

Similarly, the path of parenting is clear and the way you proceed on that path determines to a great extent what your children are going to be and do in their lives. Your way and your path will be determined by your priorities. If your priorities are aligned with the compass of God's Word, you will have the most important ingredients to help bring out the winner in your child. If not, your best efforts will prove futile; it is impossible to lead your child to a place where you have never been yourself. You may be able to share with your child the stories of other great men and women who have traveled that path, but you will never be able to lead your child unless you are on the path too. Only then will you be able to experience what I call the joy of the journey.

THE WINNER'S FOCUS

1. How would you describe yourself: as a mule, a Shetland pony, or a thoroughbred? How would you describe your child?
2. Why do you think thoroughbreds like to run with thoroughbreds, and Shetlands with Shetlands?
3. What is the true compass you are using to guide your life? On a scale of one to ten (ten = excellent, one = poor), how reliable is it?
4. Why do you think it is so difficult for most of us to admit that we have taken the wrong road at times in life?
5. If you had the power to choose, which would be more important to you: the health and happiness of your child or having your name on the tallest skyscraper in the world? How do you express that value to your child?

6. If someone asked your child to describe two things about you that your child will never forget, what two things would he or she describe?
7. In what ways is the course you are on currently the course you hope your child will emulate? In what ways do you hope your child's course will differ from your own?

15

The Joy of the Journey

I WAS SITTING in the office of Dr. Robert Schuller, pastor of the internationally known Crystal Cathedral in Garden Grove, California. We were preparing to step out onto the platform of that magnificent church for Dr. Schuller's broadcasted worship service on his television program, *The Hour of Power,* viewed by millions each week. It is easy to be overwhelmed in such an exciting environment. In the course of our conversation, I said to Dr. Schuller, "You are doing so much to help so many people here. We are trying to do what you do, only on a much smaller scale."

Dr. Schuller rose from where he was sitting, pointed his finger directly at me, and said, in his inimitable booming voice, "John, do not ever say that again! Only God can know how many apples are in one seed. Your children will marry and produce other children, who will marry and produce other children. The generations are the fruit of the seed."

I have thought about Dr. Schuller's words many times since that day, often in regard to my own family and the work that we feel called to do at Big Oak Ranch. Who would have ever thought that the horrible tragedy of my sister's death could have been the seed that God used to help more than thirteen hundred children at the Ranch over the years, and thousands of other children as the impact of our work has broadened?

My mama was in such shock she did not cry for three months after Lisa's death. She told me it took her twenty-five years before she quit asking God, "Why? Why did this happen? Why did Lisa have to die?" We may never know exactly why, but we do know that God brought good into our lives even through this tragedy. The Bible says, "And as for you, you meant evil against me, but God meant it for good in order to bring about this present result, to preserve many people alive" (Genesis 50:20). What was tragedy was also a catalyst to bring about God's plan for Big Oak Ranch, a place where hundreds of other children could have a chance to live.

When I was playing football at the University of Alabama, before every game Coach Bryant gathered our team together and said, "Gentlemen, there will be four or five plays that will determine the outcome of this ball game. You will not know when they are coming. It might be a third-down-and-two-yards-to-go situation, and we must have a first down. Or, it might be a fourth-down, goal-to-go situation. I cannot tell you in advance what the crucial plays will be. But those plays will be the turning points of this ball game. Those plays will determine whether we win or lose.

"Right now, you don't know whether you are going to be the hero or the goat; you don't know whether you are going to perform well under pressure or whether you will embarrass yourself in front of thousands of people here in the stands and the millions more watching on television. But be sure, gentlemen, those plays will come. And the only way you can be ready for them is to give your best on every play. Now, let's go do it."

In my life, my sister Lisa's death was surely one of those life-changing plays. Often in my travels and speaking, I will ask grown men and women, "What were the four or five plays that most influenced your life for good or evil?" I have yet to meet someone who could not complete the list. Sometimes the memories are deeply painful:

"The day my dad looked at me and said, 'I am going away,' and I never saw him again."

"The day my eight-year-old daughter got hit by a car and died instantly."

At other times, the memories are special moments indelibly impressed upon our minds:

"The day my dad taught me how to hit a ball."

"The time my mom saved my life by pushing me out of the way of a falling plate glass window."

"The time I made cookies with my mom."

"The times I went bike riding with my dad."

"The day I got married."

"The moment our first baby was born."

A POUCH FULL OF DIAMONDS

One of the most priceless gifts you can give your children is the special memories of things you and they have done together. These are memory diamonds. You can never know for sure where your child might find one; diamonds are often hidden in the most unusual places. I like to think of our parenting journey as an ongoing opportunity for our children to find diamonds and for parents to place them in their memory pouches.

What sort of memories are your children going to have of you? Long after your active parenting days are over, when their bags are packed and they are out on their own, what will your children think about your example? Will they say, "That is my mom. That is my dad. That is what it means to be a person of integrity. And that is the kind of person I want to be. Mom and Dad did their job."

I heard the story of George Jaeger:

It was late afternoon when the boat's engine sputtered, stalled, and refused to restart. Gallons of water surged into the craft as it pitched on sickening, six-foot swells. The five Jaegers had done all they knew to do, but it wasn't enough. An exciting fishing trip was now a thing of horror. They were going under.

Grim-faced, George Jaeger, his three sons, and his elderly father methodically tightened the buckles on their life jackets, tied themselves together with a rope, and slipped silently into a black and boiling Atlantic.

George glanced at his watch as the boat finally disappeared—6:30 p.m. Very little was said. It grew dark. First one boy and then another swallowed too much saltwater, gagged, and strangled on the brine as they fought to keep their heads up. The helpless father heard his sons, one by one, and then his dad choke and drown. But George couldn't surrender. After eight nightmarish hours, he staggered onto the shore, still pulling the rope that bound him to the bodies of the other four. Pause and try to imagine the sight!

"I realize they were all dead—my three boys and my father—but I guess I didn't want to accept it, so I kept swimming all night long," he later told reporters. "My youngest boy, Clifford, was the first to go. I had always taught our children not to fear death because it was being with Jesus Christ." Before Cliff died, his dad heard him say, "I'd rather be with Jesus than go on fighting."

In that vivid Atlantic memory, George Jaeger had a chance to witness the impact of his fifteen years as a father. The boys died quietly, with courage and dignity. Up to the very last minute, one by one they modeled the truth passed on by their father: When under pressure, stay calm . . . think . . . even if death is near, keep under control. So they did, and so they died. When the ultimate test was administered in an angry sea, they handed in perfect scores.[1]

Is that you, Dad? Is that you, Mom? It doesn't have to be.

Part of the joy of parenting is that you know where you are going and you are pointing your child in the right direction along with you. Not just in the near future, not just in regard to a career or a marriage, but in the most important issue of all: forever. The joy we experience when we get to heaven, one of these days, is going to be incomprehensible. Our family relationships here in this life are meant to get us ready for our larger family, our eternal family, which we will enjoy in heaven.

This life is tough at times, but it is not meant to be drudgery. Raising your child to be a winner can be frustrating at times, but it is not meant to be overwhelming. You should be able to know and experience the joy of the journey.

THE MOST IMPORTANT KEY
You've read this book, searching for secrets that will help you bring out the winner in your child. You've asked yourself questions, and I hope you have found some practical ideas you can

use in your relationship with your child. But please do not miss the most important key of all. It is the key that will help you find joy in the journey.

As I said right at the beginning, I am not an expert. Nor am I a perfect person; I have failed many times and have not always been all that I was supposed to be. But God forgives and eagerly welcomes us when we have a desire to get back on track.

All I can tell you is what works. At Big Oak Ranch, and in my relationships with Tee, Reagan, and Brodie, and in my personal life, what works is a relationship with God. Trusting in Jesus Christ and living according to the Bible works. I've staked my life on it. In fact, I've staked my life on *Him*.

Perhaps you have tried to find the answer in other ways and have not been able to find satisfaction. I am not surprised. Why? Because God created you and you will never be the winner He made you to be without a relationship with Him. The brilliant French mathematician and philosopher Blaise Pascal put it this way: Within every person is a God-shaped vacuum that can only be filled by Jesus Christ. Nothing or nobody else will fill that void in your life or the lives of your children. Only Jesus Christ can truly satisfy the longings of your inner person, your soul.

I speak to and work with people around the country who have every conceivable religious belief, and I have met people who claim to have no religious beliefs at all. I don't try to convince anyone that he is wrong and I am right. I don't argue about religion. Religion is, after all, merely man's search for God. I like to talk about a relationship—a relationship with Jesus Christ. Like I said, all I know is what works, and a relationship with Jesus Christ really works! If it didn't, I would not waste your time or mine.

One time, after I had spoken on this subject, a college student approached me and said, "I don't believe any of the stuff you are saying about God and Jesus and an afterlife. I think this life is all there is. When you are dead, that's it. It's over."

"You might be right," I said. "But when our earthly life is over and we face eternity, if we find out there is no life after death, neither of us has lost a thing. If I am right and there is an afterlife and Jesus is the only way to heaven, as He said, then you have lost everything!"

Whether you are a religious person or not, that God-shaped vacuum that Pascal described is still there in your life unless you have a relationship with Christ. Making money will not fill that hole. Material possessions will not satisfy your soul. Country club memberships, awards, honors, or degrees on your wall will all leave you empty. Drugs, alcohol, or sex cannot dull the ache in your heart if that void is not filled by Christ. Perhaps you are like me and you have tried many of these things, and yet still the emptiness remains within your heart. Only Jesus Christ can fill that spot in your life. Amazingly, when you trust Christ at the center of your life, it is so much easier to prioritize the many details of your life. As Pascal put it, "Jesus Christ is the center of all and the goal to which all tends." That's because when you know Christ, you can see what really matters, those things that are most important—your relationship with God, your relationship with your mate, and your relationships with your children.

Practically speaking, we have seen marked, measurable, positive changes take place in our children at Big Oak Ranch when they have discovered a genuine relationship with Christ. Helping our children find and establish biblically based spiritual values is the secret ingredient to our success at bringing out the winner in our children at Big Oak Ranch. Nothing else—no social program, no motivational program, no course in self-esteem—does for our children what Jesus does. He gives them a reason to live. He gives them unconditional love. And He gives them joy in their journey.

Please understand: You need not be a member of a dysfunctional family to need the Lord; you don't need to be morally bankrupt or intellectually stymied to realize that there is a part of you that can never be satisfied apart from a relationship with God. For those who might disagree, again, all we can do is point you to over thirteen hundred examples of how these principles can and do work in the lives of children and parents. We have seen how God can work wonders time and again in children's lives. We have seen firsthand how a little boy comes to us with "shark eyes," but by being introduced to Jesus, his life is changed because he knows someone loves him and believes in him. If you are looking for something (*Someone*, actually!) that will work in your life and the life of your child, you owe it to yourself and to your child to examine what it means to have a relationship with Jesus Christ.

We can put nice clothes on our children; we can give them a beautiful place to live, bigger television sets with more channels, fancy cars for them to drive. We can put them in the best schools, enroll them in the most prestigious extracurricular activities, and then send them off to the best colleges in the country. But if we fail to give our children the one most important key to life—life here and life forever—we will have failed in the most crucial part of the job we were created to do.

Everything else about this life is going to pass away. Only our relationship with God, or our lack of one, will last forever.

In case you haven't noticed, the odds of getting out of this world alive are pretty slim. So far, death has a perfect record. Every person who is born eventually dies. The big question is: What then?

I can answer that for you (not because I'm so smart, but because I have read and believe the Bible). One day, no matter who you are, whether you have been rich or poor, you are going to stand before God. Think of it like this: When you die, you will knock on heaven's door. God, the Ultimate Host, answers.

He will not ask you what religion you were. He will not ask whether you were white or black. He will not even ask you about all the good things you may have done. He will not ask you whether you were a good parent or whether you were the best you should have been to your marriage partner. Nor will He ask about how productive you were in this life and what you have contributed to the environment and to future generations.

He is going to examine you with only one question: "Did you accept or reject My Son, Jesus?"

HOW TO START AGAIN

How do you establish and maintain a relationship with Christ? Just going to church won't do it for you. As the late singer Keith Green used to say, going to church will not make you into a Christian any more than going to McDonald's will make you into a hamburger. You have to trust Jesus with your life. The Bible calls it faith. Put your faith in Jesus Christ—not information about Him, but the real, live person of Christ.

If you think you have exhausted all opportunities, you haven't. If you think all is lost and you have tried everything in your power to fix your family, allow me to introduce you to my friend Jesus Christ. He can fix your family, and He will start by fixing you, but you must allow Him to do so.

What must you do? You can start by believing. The Bible says:

If you confess with your mouth Jesus as Lord, and believe in your heart that God raised Him from the dead, you shall be saved; for with the heart man believes, resulting in righteousness, and with the mouth he confesses, resulting in salvation. For the Scripture says, "Whoever believes in Him will not be disappointed." (Romans 10:9–11)

Beyond that, the apostle Paul once told a frightened, frustrated fellow, who had just experienced an earthquake in his life, "Believe in the Lord Jesus, and you shall be saved, you and your household" (Acts 16:31). God does not only want you to be a winner. He wants your child to be a winner as well.

Pete Maravich was one of the premier professional basketball players in the history of the NBA. No one could shoot like Pete. No one looked like Pistol Pete, with his floppy long hair and his floppy white socks. He was the stuff legends are made of. At the age of thirty-three, he retired early from his NBA career because of a knee injury. Pete was inducted into the NBA Hall of Fame on May 5, 1987.

Known as rowdy, for Pete retirement was not easy, especially after living twenty-six years for the game. For two years he remained in seclusion, rarely making any public appearances and staying as far from basketball as he could.

Maravich later wrote:

The time gave me more opportunity to ponder my existence and question the huge void left in my life since walking away from the game I worshiped. I began trying to fill the emptiness with my family, especially my two-year-old son Jaeson. I figured if I could be father of the year and husband of the year, I could find the happiness and peace of mind I longed for. . . .

It wasn't until I started throwing myself into Jaeson's world that I realized how much being a role model could affect my son. I knew my drinking could be a stumbling block, and it was the first thing abolished from our home life. But it was hypocritical to clean up things inside our home, such as alcohol, when I continued drinking outside. . . . I felt that money and things it could buy in this world were my tickets to pleasure and happiness. But even with all the money, I was miserable. Deep down I knew life had to be more than parties, a Mercedes, and stocks and bonds.

I had the money and I had the time, but with too much of both on my hands, I drove Jackie [his wife] crazy with wild ideas and strange obsessions. . . . I couldn't tell how paranoid and fatalistic about my future I was becoming, and I couldn't see the unsettled individual I had become since leaving basketball. Questions about my purpose in life bombarded me: "Why am I here? What were all the years in basketball about, especially since they turned out so empty?" My mind was full of hard questions, but with all my searching, I found no answers. . . . The fame and fads were all temporary and fleeting! My exploration of different religions, astrology, astronomy, nutrition, UFO's, and even basketball only revealed all the more an emptiness I couldn't fill.

I became a desperate man, facing the inevitable questions each person must face: "What do I have to live for? What value do I have? What will happen to me when I die?" I hadn't found a purpose anywhere in a past filled with success, fame, and fortune. For a man that seemed to have it all, in my estimation, I had no purpose, no reason for being.

The course my life had taken through the years

had always clashed with the way God had intended, and it was time to admit it. I cried out to God, saying, "I've cursed you and I've spit on you. I've mocked you and used your name in vain. I've kicked, punched, and laughed at you. Oh, God, can you forgive me, can you forgive me? Please, save me, please. I've had it with this life of mine. I've had it with all the world's answers for happiness. All of it, the money, fame, and things have left me so empty. . . .

I prayed a simple prayer as best I could. "Jesus Christ, come into my life . . . forgive me of my sin. I believe with all my heart that you died for me and rose from the grave so I would have eternal life. Make me the person you want me to be."

Through this simple act of surrender, the void that once loomed so large was filled. From that moment on, my life was never to be the same. The transformation in my life was astonishing. Because of my new-found faith a new Pete had miraculously emerged with joy and a purpose for meaningful existence. My family could hardly believe they were seeing the same person they had known. I finally knew there was a reason for my being alive, and the assurance translated peace into my face and my attitude.[2]

Pistol Pete's conversion took place in 1982. He became a solid Christian man and a better husband and father. In January of 1988, Pete was playing in a pickup basketball game at the First Nazarene Church of Pasadena gymnasium when suddenly he collapsed with a heart attack. Pistol Pete Maravich lay dying in the arms of Dr. James Dobson, who was on the court that day.

Dr. Dobson was profoundly affected by Pete's death. The psychologist went home and told his son, Ryan, "This is a lesson we need to learn. We never know how much time we have. If I go before you, just tell me that you will be there."

How about you, Mom and Dad? Are you going to be there for your child?

A father asked his little girl if she knew where heaven was located. Without blinking an eye, the little girl said, "Heaven is wherever you are, Daddy."

Where are you, Dad? Where are you, Mom?

Are you on your way to being there in heaven? Are you pointing the way to heaven for your child? Come, join us in the joy of the journey!

Great success in every other area of life will never compensate for the awful sense of loss you will experience if you know you have lost the joy of the journey in raising your child. But there is no need to lose. We can win! It is guaranteed. And we can help bring out the winner in our children. Let's not settle for being less than the best parents we can be. Allow the Lord to help you bring out the winner in your child!

THE WINNER'S FOCUS

1. What are the five "plays" that have most influenced your life positively or negatively?
2. In what ways has God brought good out of a situation in your family that looked at first like a tragedy or a failure?
3. Try to recall the circumstances surrounding some of the precious diamonds in your memory pouch. What are some of the diamonds you hope your child has safely secured in her memory pouch?
4. Why do you think some people try so many other types of answers before they come to the truth about a relationship with Jesus Christ?

5. How can a strong faith in God help you in setting boundaries for your child, disciplining your child, and charting a safe, productive course in life?

6. What is the most important insight you have received as a result of reading this book? How do you plan to put that insight to work in your life? How will it help you bring out the winner in your child?

Notes

Chapter 3

1. Tim Hansel, *What Kids Need Most in a Dad* (Old Tappan, NJ: Revell, 1984),45–46.

2. Gary Smalley, *The Hidden Value of a Man* (Dallas, TX: Word, 1994), 25–27.

Chapter 4

1. Henry Cloud and John Townsend, *Boundaries* (Grand Rapids: Zondervan, 1992), 173.

Chapter 5

1. Larry Christenson, *The Christian Family* (Minneapolis: Bethany Fellowship, 1970), 66–67.

2. Charles Stanley, *How to Keep Your Kids on Your Team* (Nashville: Thomas Nelson, 1986), 87.

Chapter 7

1. Christenson, *Christian Family*, 90–91.

Chapter 8

1. James Dobson, *Hide or Seek* (Old Tappan: Revell, 1979), 95.

Chapter 9

1. Zig Ziglar, *Raising Positive Kids in a Negative World* (Nashville: Thomas Nelson, 1985), 150–51.

2. Larry Poland, *The Mediator*, 10 (1995).

3. Stormie Omartian, *The Power of a Praying Parent* (Eugene: Harvest House, 1995), 63.

Chapter 11

1. Zig Ziglar, *Raising Positive Kids in a Negative World*, 116–17.

Chapter 13

1. James Dobson, *Dare to Discipline* (Wheaton: Tyndale, 1994), 194–95.

2. David B. Peters, *Betrayal of Innocence* (Waco: Word, 1986), 93.

Chapter 15

1. Charles R. Swindoll, *Man to Man* (New York: Harper Collins, 1996), 35.

2. Pete Maravich and Darrel Campbell, *Heir to a Dream* (Nashville: Thomas Nelson, 1987), 187–94.

JOHN CROYLE is a graduate of the University of Alabama, a second-team All-America football star, the founder of the Big Oak Ranch, and a motivational speaker who is in demand nationwide. His story has been featured in *Reader's Digest, Sports Illustrated, People,* and *Focus on the Family* magazine. He has made guest appearances on NBC's *Today,* CNN News, ABC Sports' *HalfTime Report,* Robert Schuller's *Hour of Power,* and *The 700 Club.* He lives near Gadsden, Alabama, with his wife, Tee, and their children, Reagan and Brodie.

KEN ABRAHAM has written several *New York Times* bestsellers, including *Zinger,* the autobiography of Paul Azinger. Other recent successful books include *I Was Wrong: The Jim Bakker Story* and *The Gamer,* with Major League baseball player Gary Carter. Current projects include *Who Are the Promise Keepers?* (Harper) and *Tender Road Home,* with Susie Luchsinger, sister of Reba McEntire.